THE KING OF VIOLINS

THE EXTRAORDINARY LIFE OF MA SICONG, CHINA'S GREATEST VIOLIN VIRTUOSO

M.G.CRISCI and
CHENG KEN CHI Ph.D.

In collaboration with IDA CHI Ph.D. and NINA CHI SABINS Ph.D.

ORCA PUBLISHING COMPANY USA | 2020

Also by M.G. Crisci

7 Days in Russia
Call Sign, White Lily
Donny and Vladdy
Ergonia, Land of the Giant Ants
Indiscretion
Mary Jackson Peale
Only in New York, Volume 1
Only in New York, Volume 2
Papa Cado
Project Zebra
Salad Oil King
Save the Last Dance
She Said. He Said.
Still Standing
The King of Violins
This Little Piggy

Learn more at
mgcrisci.com
amazon.com/M.G.Crisci/e/B003509QRK
twitter.com/worldofmgcrisci
YouTube.com/worldofmgcrisci
Facebook.com/worldofmgcrisci

Published by Orca Publishing Company, USA
Formatted by http://www.eBookIt.com
Last update: November 23, 2021

ISBN-13: 978-1-4566-3506-0 (ebook)
ISBN-13: 978-1-4566-3552-7 (paperback)
ISBN-13: 978-1-4566-3534-3 (hardcover)

Edited by Robin Friedman and Holly Scudero

Cover design by Good World Media

Pictures courtesy of Ma Sicong Library, Guangzhou, China,
and the Ma Sicong family archives, USA

First Edition

Table of Contents

再見老毛

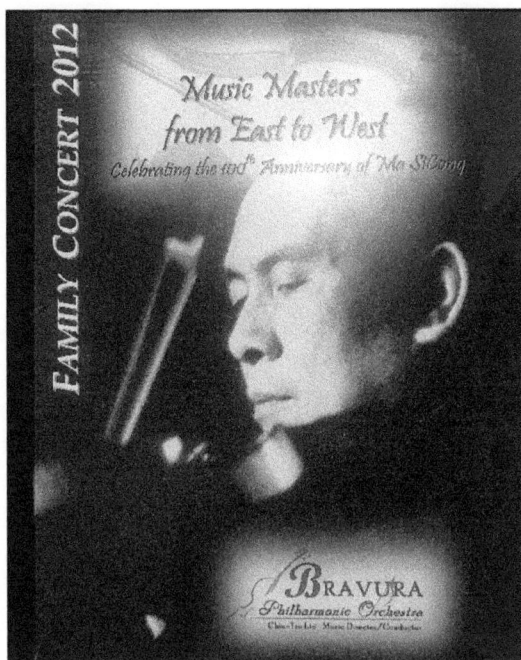

Music Masters
from East to West
Celebrating the 100th Anniversary of Ma SiCong

FAMILY CONCERT 2012

BRAVURA
Philharmonic Orchestra

馬思聰

May 7, 1912 – May 20, 1978

*"You are pure as pearl,
but suffered dirt covering.
You are a national treasure,
but was ravaged.
A wiseman exiled,
but anguish persisted
Fainted music of love,
drifts across the ocean.
Music of China,
forever green summer or winter.
centuries' aroma,
last to the end of time."*

Foreword

前言

As the author of 16 very different books across multiple genres, I always get asked the same question: "Where do the ideas for your stories come from?" My reply is always the same: real life and some version of fate. *The King of Violins* is no different.

I'm the son of Italian American immigrants; I was born, raised, and lived most of my life in New York. I have no Chinese ties and a few Chinese acquaintances.

This book started some years back with my friend John, an Italian American from Philadelphia. From time to time, we'd have coffee and talk about life. One day, he announced he had fallen in love with a Chinese American named Ida. We attended the wedding, and, as friends do, stayed in touch. One day, over coffee, he said, "I think I have a pretty major storyline for you."

As a New Yorker, I was skeptical; as a friend, I listened. John told me he, his wife, and his father-in-law, Ken, had just returned from China, where they attended a museum dedication and elaborate government ceremony to honor Ida's grandfather, violinist, and composer Ma Sicong. John said Ken had read my best-selling book *Call Sign, White Lily*, about a Russian teenager Lilia Litvyak, who was the world's first female fighter pilot. John said Ken had the first draft of a book about Ma and was looking for some constructive help.

My first response was negative. "John, do you know how much work goes into understanding another culture to create that kind of book?" My second response was equally negative, "What the hell makes the story of a violin player all that interesting? Sounds like an academic bore." John persisted. He mumbled something about a 21-

gun salute, presidential suites in Beijing, a daring escape from the Cultural Revolution. Reluctantly, I acquiesced. With due respect to Ken, the draft read like an inward-looking personal diary. I was now sure—a project like this would be time-consuming, boring, and have no commercial appeal.

A few weeks later, John attended his mother's funeral in Florida and was killed instantly by a car that blindsided him. I knew fate was at it again.

Uncertain of what the final product might look like, I agreed to partner with Ken on the venture. I quickly learned Ma Sicong was a great violinist and composer with a body of work that rivals that of Mozart, Brahms, and Beethoven. His roller-coaster through the mysterious world of Chinese society made him a hero of the common man, and a major public relations embarrassment to Mao Zedong. His eventual escape to the United States, like the opera Lakme', was a story within the story.

Thank you for selecting our book. Ken and I hope you'll enjoy it. When you're finished, I suspect you'll also realize why politically balanced Chinese American relationships are a long, long way from the finish line.

M. G. Crisci

Introduction

介绍

Today, Chinese violinist and composer Ma Sicong (pronounced *Ma-se-tung*) is revered as *The King of Violins* in his native China. Despite those recent accolades, life has not been kind to Ma.

Ma was born in 1912 in the Chinese province of Guangdong, (uqn-sow) a coastal area bordered by Hong Kong and Macau.

Life in China has never been easy. The past 5,000 years has seen the rise of well-intentioned dynasties that make numerous societal contributions and then crumble—centuries later—under the force of their corruption and an insatiable appetite to maintain power. As China's final ruling dynasty, the Qing, crumbled at the beginning of the twentieth century, China became ripe for the expansion of foreign imperialism; a violent, roller-coaster transition into a united Republic of China; the imposition of state-controlled communism; and the elimination of individual rights and freedoms as decadent bourgeois musings.

In 1967, Ma and his family said, "Jai Jian" (goodbye) to their beloved homeland and fled to America to avoid certain imprisonment during the self-appointed supreme leader Mao Zedong's (mao-ze-dong) Cultural Revolution. As you will learn, the family's flight to freedom was filled with danger and uncertainty.

Ma and his family lived in New York initially before subsequently settling in Philadelphia. He continued to compose and perform until he died in 1987.

A consequence of his self-imposed exile: his creative genius is unknown to all but a few classical aficionados in China. As you are about to discover, his musical artistry and 57 symphonic compositions, ballets, and operas place him in the company of the world's greatest composers, such as Bach, Brahms, Mozart, and violinist virtuosos Niccolò Paganini, Itzhak Perlman, and Isaac Stern, among others.

The King of Violins is the first-ever *politically neutral* book written about the inspirational accomplishments and inhumane atrocities experienced by this Chinese musical icon. Great care has been taken to make this book painstakingly accurate. Much of the material is based on actual conversations of Ma and from memories, notes, papers, and picture archives of Ma's son-in-law, Cheng Ken Chi, Ph.D., and his granddaughters, Ida Chi, Ph.D., and Nina Chi Sabins Ph.D. You will become privy to certain family matters—some good, some bad—that have never appeared in print. Some in China may wish to disagree or even protest these facts, but the truth is the truth.

To make Ma's life story more reader-friendly, we have written the book in *first-person Ma*. The family and I are confident Ma would have liked his story shared in that manner. He died frustrated that much written about him in his native China was filled with inaccuracies, lies, and propaganda.

~

Ma's dreams were grand but straightforward. He hoped his life's work would serve as an inspiration to struggling artists around the world to never stop dreaming big dreams. Ma knew creativity and imagination were virtues to be cultivated and revered.

He also hoped his musical legacy would, in some small way, increase the cultural understanding and mutual trust between his homeland, China, and his adopted home, the United States of America.

~

One final comment before you begin your journey. To better understand Ma's beliefs, actions, music, and life choices, you will need to understand some of China's complicated, mysterious past. A musical genius who loved his country does not wake up one morning at the age of 55 and decide to leave under the cloak of darkness.

Every attempt has been made to integrate selected historical passages in an approachable manner. Nevertheless, those passages are not meant to be an all-encompassing academic treatise and should not be judged as such. The two items at the end of the book—the *Afterword* and *Ma's Photo Album*—offer further insights into one extraordinary life.

Also, to make this book more-reader friendly, the first time a Chinese name appears, it is followed by the phonetic pronunciation of that word in English. We have avoided the exclusive use of native Chinese characters.

Chapter 1.

My Father and Mother

我的父母

(l.) Ma's father, Ma Yuhanng(ma-you-hang), was a scholar and revolutionary thinker. (r.) Ma's mother, Huang Chuliang, (who-am-chuly-an) was a housewife, singer, and storyteller.

I wish to begin my story by telling you a little about my father and mother. My father was more than just a great man; he was an important influence on my life choices and passed on to me his gifts of determination and love of country. My mother was my moral compass and gave me her love of music.

To better understand my father's and mother's principles and beliefs, you need to understand a little of the times in which they were born and raised.

As I have come to understand over my lifetime, we are all, to one extent or another, a product of the environment in which we live and the individual experiences we have as human beings.

~

My father, Ma Yuhanng, was born in 1883 in Haifeng (hi-fang), a small sea village on the South China seashore, in Canton Province. Today, Haifeng is known as Guangdong. He came from a middle-class family, which in China meant they had just enough money to live. Father had two brothers: one three years older, the other three years younger. When my father was 13, his father passed away suddenly, leaving the three brothers responsible for earning money to support the family.

As a young man, my father grew up during the final stages of the Qing Dynasty (*Cing*), which had ruled China from 1644 to 1911. The physically violent Qing minority was the last of the ten Imperial dynasties that ruled my homeland for almost 3,000 years. They employed fear, corruption, and unilateral legal mandates to control my country's largest ethnic group, called the Han, a gentle people who still represent more than 90 percent of the Chinese population.

During the reign of the Qings, they always reminded the Han that they were fortunate to be ruled by "intellectually superior" Manchurians. The marginalization of the peasant class led to bloody wars and perennial unrest. Ironically, the Qings also left a legacy of amazing achievements in art, culture, and economics.

Long before my father was born, the Chinese population in the provinces grew from 130 million to 400 million, placing a severe strain on food supplies. To eliminate the possibility of famine and significant social upheaval, the Qings decided to increase agricultural yield in China's fertile north by forcing the Han to use new fertilizers and advanced irrigation techniques imported from Western Europe.

The Qings also declared that the profits from these higher yields would be shared exclusively among the Manchurian minority.

Initially, the indigenous Han farmers worked for the Qings while quietly expressing their frustration at 150 years of marginalization. One of the ways the Qings maintained control during these chaotic times was to promote the value of scholarly pursuit among the peasant class by establishing the Imperial Examination. Candidates who passed the exam received the title of "Scholar" to reinforce their intellectual superiority to the Han peasant masses. My grandfather was considered a Scholar, and his family was considered a prominent member of the Qing Dynasty.

To complete the Imperial Examination, you were required to read many books of literature and write a thesis that explained the benefits of these stories to the Qing Dynasty. The idea was to recognize Scholars publicly.

~

As a young man, my father and his best friend, Cheng Jiongming (*cheng-jo-ming*), decided to stay in the good graces of the ruling class by becoming trusted scholars. At the same time, they found a creative way to profit from the examination process by obtaining a fee for helping other students pass their own Imperial Examinations.

My father and Cheng would hide outside a window of the examination room while their student wrote the test composition subject on a piece of paper. The student would then roll the paper into a small ball and throw it to them. My father would pick up the document, run and hide behind a nearby building, correct the composition, and then smuggle it back to the waiting student.

While my father realized helping others to cheat on the Imperial exam was not honorable, his activities did generate extra money for his family. To Father, that purpose was noble!

In 1898, both Father, age 15, and Cheng, 20, passed the Imperial Examinations at the county level and earned the titles of Xia Cai (*ca-hi*) meaning scholar or skillful writers.

~

4

In 1903, my father married my mother when they were both 20 years old; ventually, our family numbered ten children—six girls and four boys. As a child, my mother, also the product of a peasant family, planted the rice fields and helped her older brother gather grass and wood on the mountain for cooking and heat. Because she performed these chores as a child, my mother was spared from the barbaric tradition of foot binding.

My mother had a kind heart, a tolerant and forgiving attitude, and a quick, smart mind. Although a peasant at birth, she turned into an elegant, graceful, and highly resourceful young woman. She managed the family budget; repaired water faucets and broken chairs; and fixed household electrical problems while my father disappeared for months at a time chasing revolutionary social change.

Mother also taught my sisters and brothers about moral standards and values. While technically illiterate, she had a detailed memory. She passed along stories from the ancient Chinese morality book *Three Character Classic* and *The Ballad of Mulan* that her mother had taught her. I have vivid memories of her sitting by the fire, explaining, "People at birth are naturally good. Their natures are similar, but their habits make them different." She also told us to study and work hard. "No particular skill will make you a beggar."

~

Besides my father's dissatisfaction with the behavior of the ruling class, he held advanced views about the role of women in what was an entirely male-dominated society. He felt women should not be at a disadvantage to men in reading or writing and organized a school in his home to eliminate illiteracy among the women in his village. He was also a strict disciplinarian; no one dared to be late for class.

Father insisted my mother attend the classes and complete homework assignments like all the other women, even though she was breastfeeding, cooking, and running the household. In time, she learned to read, write, and sing local operas, such as *The Butterfly Lovers* (a Chinese *Romeo and Juliet*). She was also quite the performer. She made people laugh during the comical moments and shed tears when the opera saddened.

While I loved and respected my father as a teacher, he was also an intimidating presence at home. He would order my brothers and sisters to study hard, then sit and watch over us as we worked. When I protested, my father became even more strict.

Chapter 2.

Father's Best Friend

父亲最好的朋友

Ma's father's best friend was the revolutionary hero Cheng Jiongming.

Although my father and Cheng were born in the same town five years apart, their formative years were quite different. Cheng's father was a landlord of moderate wealth, and Cheng was sent to a private school to study Confucian classics at the age of six.

Cheng trained to be a schoolteacher at the advanced Haifeng Normal School. After graduating, he was banned from teaching because his radical ideas were deemed to be at odds with the "best intentions" of the Qings, who were desperate to maintain power.

Soon, my father and Cheng reunited as classmates at Guangdong Academy of Law and Political Science. This Qing-sanctioned institution was created to demonstrate the Dynasty's willingness to support new ideas that would improve the Han quality of life.

In 1899, the friends graduated at the top of their class, frustrated that the Han majority had allowed the Qings to "carve China up like a melon." Both men believed the solution to centuries of social unrest was a unified Republic of China that served all the people. They had witnessed the bloody anti-imperialist, anti-foreign, anti-Christian uprising known as the Boxer Rebellion, which ravaged the country for more than two years, despite the Han joining forces with the Qings. When the rebellion was lost, they were appalled at the terms of the surrender agreement.

The British, French, Russian, American, and German invaders created a series of so-called "unequal treaties" that effectively reduced the Chinese provinces to a collection of colonies managed by corrupt Chinese provincial officials who reported to the Western powers. This patchwork of enclaves came to be known as *spheres of influence*, places where foreign merchants maintained unlimited access to valuable Chinese natural resources such as tea, silks, porcelain, and decorative luxuries. Generally, the foreigners paid corrupt officials for the goods with uncut opium (80 percent or higher heroin purity), which created severe addiction and unfettered demand among the Han majority.

Determined by what they saw, Cheng and my father wanted their homeland returned to its rightful owners. They used their vacations from Law School to return to Haifeng to promote the benefits of self-government, the eradication of opium smoking, the improvement of local grain depots, and the creation of nurseries for children, so older family members could earn more money.

After graduation, the two friends opened China's first private school of self-government, Haifeng Local Zhizhi Hui (*hi-fong-ze-ze-way*), designed to create modern social thinking. They also published a self-government newspaper *Haifeng Zhizhi Bao* (*hi-fong-ze-ze-bao*), which proposed revolutionary ideas such as equal rights for all classes. They also advocated the elimination of outdated, unproductive Chinese traditions. For example, they suggested men cut off their ponytails—long a symbol of the Qing Dynasty masculine superiority.

~

The intensely patriotic Cheng realized words alone would not change centuries-old behavior—there needed to be a grassroots likeminded revolutionary force. Cheng persuaded over thirty young men from Haifeng—including my father—to swear secret support for a national revolution. To reinforce the importance of their endeavor, Cheng made the group complete their pledge of allegiance in front of the portrait of Wen Tianxiang (*when te-ent-tiam*), whom the masses had long considered China's greatest patriot.

Wen's iconic status was created during the fall of the Song Dynasty in the thirteenth century. Grand Chancellor Wen was captured by the invading Mongol armies of Kublai Khan. He was offered an important post in the new ruling Yuan Dynasty if he convinced the remaining Song military forces to surrender. Wen rejected the offer to work for a government he viewed as barbaric and immoral; instead, he preferred to practice the Confucian virtues of benevolence and righteousness learned in his youth. He suffered four years in a Yuan military prison before he was beheaded in 1283.

His last written words referenced the legacy of truth: "All men are mortal, but my loyalty will illuminate the annals of history forever."

~

Despite Cheng's zeal, China continued to deteriorate in the hands of foreigners. Cheng and my father joined multiple revolutionary movements dedicated to overthrowing the Qing and extracting China from foreign intrusion. They believed, as did their hero Wen, that one must prefer to sacrifice one's own life than abandon one's principles. Thanks to my father, I would live my own life that way.

In 1909, the two friends joined Sun Yat-sen's Revolutionary Alliance for Democracy, which was predicated on three core principles: nationalism, democracy, and the right of people to earn a fair wage.

Two years later, my father and Cheng joined the Sina Assassination Team in Hong Kong. Cheng was named a team leader, and my father agreed to the dangerous mission of smuggling explosives back into Guangdong Province by fastening them to his own body. My oldest brother, Siqui, who also was staunchly anti-Qing, traveled with my father from Macao to Guangzhou with explosives strapped to his body on two separate occasions.

Later that same year, my father was named a deputy commander of the First Revolution, which is generally recognized as the war that finally toppled the Qing dynasty in 1912 and officially put an end to 4,000 years of Chinese rule by corrupt dynasties.

Within months of the Qing collapse, the Republic of China was formed, and Sun Yat-sen was named its first President. Sun envisioned a two-phase approach to democracy. The first was to eliminate conflicting provincial beliefs by using military force to unify the country into a one-party government. Once political order was firmly established, Sun believed he could gradually introduce the selected principles of democratic human rights, regardless of class.

Cheng and my father disagreed with Sun about his two-phase strategy. They believed the fastest way to create the united Chinese Republic was to install self-governed united provinces with elected parliament members and local officials, similar to the American system of governance. Despite their differences, the two remained loyal to Sun.

To oversee unification by military force, Sun yielded power to the revolutionary commander, Yuan Shikai (pronounced *Yo-wan See-ki*), who proclaimed himself the new emperor. However, several provincial governors continued to pledge their loyalty to Sun, and soon, my country was in the midst of another leadership struggle. This struggle was commonly known as "The Second Revolution."

Chapter 3.

Life as a Kid

小孩子的生活

Ma, at the age of seven, in the family garden.

I was born in 1912 in the early days of the Sun presidency, as the fifth of ten children, some of whom I never knew very well.

My parents said I didn't show any particular interest in or talent for music as a young child. When I was about three years old, my mother said I heard music for the first time on my grandma's phonograph. I surprised and amused the entire family by spontaneously singing and dancing with great joy.

After that, memorizing and playing music came quickly. When I was seven, we were sitting at my aunt's house when she began to play Chinese music on the organ. I asked her if she would teach me. She smiled and nodded. After just a few lessons, I could play those same songs without ever looking at a music sheet. I remember the smile in my mother's eyes as she watched me play. She seemed amazed at how quickly and confidently my small hands moved around the keyboard. Neither of us understood my gifts at that moment, but she and my father decided to buy me an organ.

At nine, while I was at boarding school, I saw students playing a little instrument called a harmonica, which fit my small hands perfectly. I quickly mastered it. Later, I became fascinated with an ancient Chinese string instrument called the yueqin (*you-kin*), on which I learned to play intricate Cantonese music.

It would be three more years before I even heard a violin, much less learned how to play. Learning to play the violin was a complete accident.

~

Because of my father's revolutionary activities and exile to Southeast Asia, my mother played a significant role in developing my childhood values. She regularly recited the famous *Three Character Classic* to me and my younger brothers and sisters. In simple terms, she taught us many essential tenets of Confucian morality. Notably, people at birth are naturally good and similar—it's their habits that make them different. Secondly, respect for elders is a virtue to be cultivated.

While my mother was illiterate, her heart was pure, and her memory was rich and full. She taught me never to try to take advantage of others, to care and share things among my siblings, and to study and work hard. "If you don't have a skill in a particular field, you will become a street beggar."

While not disrespectful, I was always full of questions. Mother used to say I was her stubborn child; she was most at ease when I went to school. One day, when I was about six, my mother got an unexpected notice from my teacher. He asked her to meet him at school. When she arrived, the teacher asked, "Ma has not attended school for several days, where does he go?"

My mother was surprised and replied, "There must be some mistake. I send my son off to school every day."

"Really?" replied the teacher, who walked my mother around the school. "Do you see him anywhere?"

On the way home, my mother thought about how to educate me about the importance of following the rules. When she returned home, she acted like nothing happened that day. But the next day, after I left for school, she followed me. It was a beautiful spring day, so once I was safely out of sight, I changed direction and headed for the beach. I loved to explore all that nature had to offer. I walked a few miles to the seaside and sat quietly, observing the movements of crabs, shrimp, and other tiny sea creatures. Then I went swimming far below the water's surface to explore rock and coral formations.

One day, after I got out of the water and began to put my clothes on, my mother suddenly appeared. "Ai, you swim like a fish." (Ali was my nickname.) I didn't know what to say. She continued, "You must be hungry by now; let's go home." She reached for my hand, and we calmly walked home. When we were inside the house, my mother asked, "Can you tell me why you don't go to school for days at a time?"

I told the truth. "Mother, my teacher never smiles, and he uses a ruler to hit my palms."

"Why does he do that?"

"Because he has decided I am not following instruction like the others," I replied.

"Is he correct?"

I hesitated. "No."

My mother remained silent. She knew challenging her headstrong son would not accomplish anything. She slowly walked over to the window and called my nickname, "Ma, see the high-spirited gentlemen on the horse dressed in nice clothes?" I nodded.

"Now look over here. What do you see?" "A street beggar," I replied.

"Do you know the difference between the two men? The gentleman attended school every day so he could get a good job; the beggar did not."

The next day, my mother accompanied me to school and said to the teacher, "My son loves people that smile. Please smile more often."

Both the teacher and I got the message. I never again missed a day of school.

Chapter 4.

Friends and Enemies

朋友与敌人

(left) Ma's father's friend, Sun Yat-sen, Father of the Nation of China.
(right) My father's enemy, Yuan Shika(yea-she-pai) Renegade Emperor of China.

During the early years of Sun Yat-sen's presidency, Yuan decided to proclaim himself the Emperor of China and maintain order by establishing the first modern Chinese army. He also tried to maintain remnants of the Qing dynasty by introducing a more efficient but self-serving government in North China. To enforce these reforms, Yuan brutally crushed all dissension and made enemies of numerous provincial factions.

My father and his friend Cheng became collateral damage in the ensuing political chaos and were exiled to Southeast Asia by Yuan, where they lived for almost three years.

During this period, it became clear Sun never had power over the whole country—even his power base in Guangdong was in chaos at times. Sixteen military cliques, from the North and South Provinces —with different ideas about how and who should rule China—vied for control by military force. My father and Cheng returned to Guangzhou, where they organized the Guangzhou Salvation Army with several surrounding provinces to rebuild Sun's military might. Sun's armies were funded by successful Chinese who had left the country but remained supportive of a new Republic of China. Sun called these overseas investors "The Fathers of the Revolution." After several bloody battles, Sun's army regained control.

Sun planned to have Yuan executed for treason and corruption. But Yuan died suddenly of kidney failure (uremia) in 1916. And so began what we Chinese call *The Warlords Era*. Different provinces joined forces with like-mind forces to gain control of parts of China.

I was never interested in politics, and my father discussed little of these matters when he was home. But things changed dramatically for the better in 1920. Sun appointed Cheng as Governor of Guangdong, and Cheng made my father, now 37, the Minister of Finance. Both men valued being scholars, and the new Guangdong government quickly declared the importance of practical education to help the newly unified China grow prosperous. Chen felt he was well suited to the job of teaching Chinese merchants how to grow their businesses.

My father's new well-paying position also meant our family could now afford to send my brothers to Paris to learn new skills, which would make them valuable citizens to the United Republic of China. Siqui, 19, studied agriculture and agricultural economics; Siwu, 17, studied business and law.

~

As my brothers studied, Father's reputation as Finance Minister grew. He was considered a patriot of vision, imagination, and honesty. But as it turned out, he was also a man of generosity to a fault. One day in 1922, an unscrupulous overseas Chinese merchant who had consistently donated to the revolutionary movement approached my father. The man needed a loan of $30,000 (approximately $2 million in today's dollars) to pass the customs inspection for a variety of European goods he wanted to sell in his department store.

"That is an extraordinarily large loan," said my father.

The man responded, "Not from the government's fund." He insisted he would repay the loan in 30 days, immediately after the goods arrived and were sold. "The loan," he said, "should also generate a nice profit for the Province. Which should mean kind words for the Minister."

My father authorized a short-term bridge loan. Unfortunately, the department store plan failed as some goods "disappeared" in transit and others sold far below estimates. The man could not repay the loan. The only thing my father got for his department store mishap was the shame of a sizeable unpaid loan in his name. I didn't understand all the circumstances at the time, but it was clear the public humiliation nearly caused my mother to commit suicide. I never forgot that lesson as I got older.

My father had no choice but to repay the government fund by borrowing money from overseas relatives and friends who had fled China and its political turmoil.

Fortunately, my two older brothers had also started a business and were successfully transporting crude oil from abroad to Hong Kong, where they refined the oil and sold it to China, making a handsome profit. They helped repay my father's remaining debt to the Province and friends and family.

Eventually, my father resigned as Minister of Finance and was forced to live in Hong Kong for two years.

Chapter 5.

Studying in Paris

在巴黎学习

At 11, Ma traveled to Paris for the first time.

The first time I even heard mention of a violin was when older brother Siqui (*se-ke*) wrote home that he had decided to learn to play the violin as a hobby while studying at the university in Paris.

He planned to eventually bring the violin home to show my parents his newfound skill on an instrument virtually unknown in China at the time. But fate had other plans.

One misty afternoon in 1922, while riding home from a music lesson, he decided to physically challenge himself by riding his bicycle down a sharp slope. Unfortunately, Siqui lost control, slid off the bike, and tore his skin so severely his kneecap was exposed.

He searched for a proper doctor, first in France and then in Germany—without success—to reconstruct the knee and close the wound without causing infection. As Siqui's pain worsened, he was forced to return to Haifeng, where a little-known Chinese herbal medicine was prescribed. Miraculously, the herbal concoction worked, but the healing process took another six months.

During that time, Siqui saw the pain and sadness etched on the faces of the starving, cold Chinese peasants who struggled just to survive. He decided an academic knowledge of agricultural theory and modern agrarian technology was of little value given current conditions. When he returned to Paris, he left the Nancy School of Agriculture and changed his major to economics at Sciences Po, which combined research with practical realities.

~

During his recuperation at home, Siqui explained he couldn't attend school, so he passed the time by playing a violin in his apartment. "My practice process was awkward, but it worked. I used to place my good foot on the ground and my injured foot on a chair." Since the instrument was unfamiliar to me, I asked if he would demonstrate. Siqui tucked his violin under his chin. Suddenly the room was filled with beautiful but foreign musical notes. I was mesmerized; I sat quietly and listened. I would never forget that moment. I didn't realize at the time, but I had discovered my life's passion.

"You like the sound of my violin?" asked Siqui.

"I love it," I replied. "How did you learn to play so well?"

Siqui explained he took lessons with a teacher in Paris. "The violin is a complicated instrument that requires precision and creativity. Small changes in the use of the strings and bow can create a wide variety of notes."

Siqui's implied challenge was intriguing. "I would like to learn how to play."

"Perhaps when you are older," replied Siqui. I persisted. Siqui sensed my determination.

"Ma, that would require study in Paris. No one knows or teaches the violin in China.

"I understand," I replied. "So, take me with you when you return."

Siqui dismissed my passion as the musing of an 11-year-old boy. "Sure, Ma, when I return to Paris, I'll bring you with me to study."

We shook hands. As far as I was concerned, Siqui and I had made a deal. Not quite a year later, Siqui's injury was healed, and he was ready to return to Paris. I reminded him of our agreement.

He stared for a moment, "Are you serious?" I nodded with conviction.

He explained the issue to my mother. She shook her head, "No."

I overheard Siqui trying to debate my mother. I decided to inject myself into the conversation. "When I go to France, I'll live with Siqui in Paris and take lessons there."

Mother had her doubts; she tried to reason with me, saying, "Ma, you are only 11 years old and don't speak the language.

I remained steadfast: "I will learn."

Finally, Mother acquiesced. "Okay, but if I allow you to go, I do not want to hear you are homesick and want to come home."

~

I remember the journey to France vividly; it was my first time away from home. I was excited about the opportunity but, as you can imagine at 11 years old, I felt great insecurity about being away from my homeland, living in a place with very different customs and traditions.

We left Guangdong Harbor in a small boat that rocked in the currents and the sea breezes. Soon we changed to a bigger, ocean-ready ship. I stood on the deck, watching the mountains of my homeland get smaller and smaller. Soon there was nothing but blue sky and vast oceans. Everything felt surreal.

Siqui just stared silently. I knew something was wrong. "What is on your mind?"

He laughed. "Such an important question from one so little." He paused. "I was thinking about how the wars have left our family to struggle financially. Like Father, I hate the Qing."

One snowy day, a month later, we sailed into the Marseille Harbor, then we made our way to Paris. My first impressions of Paris were different from what I imagined. The streets were desolate, the buildings gray and dark, and there was a dense fog. For the first time, I felt homesick; I missed my home, my homeland, my parents, and my brothers and sisters. But I had no regrets because I was confident this would be the city where I would come to master the violin.

~

Initially, Siqui rented a room in a small apartment in a building in Fontainebleau, about 30 miles outside Paris. My brother was referred to a female violin teacher. I remember that first lesson as if it was yesterday. Madame arrived with what appeared to be an old violin in a worn travel case. She removed the instrument and bow with unimaginable reverence.

Madame placed the bow on the A string and gave it a pull, then said, "par ici" (this way). She handed the violin to me. I did as she did and followed her "par ici" with my "par ci." At that moment, I had no idea what I said, but the sound the violin made was rich and full, and she nodded and smiled. I assumed I had just learned my first French phrase. Siqui confirmed that later!

After the lesson, Siqui asked, "So, little brother, how was your first lesson?"

I explained the madame was pleasant enough. "But what kind of teacher teaches her students with such an old violin?"

He smiled. "You are joking, little brother!" Then he put his arm around my shoulder and explained, "Ma, you will learn that the older the violin, the mellower the sound, and the more valuable it is. In this city, you may find violins 200 years or older."

During the next few months, I would also learn that speaking French was very different from speaking Chinese and writing in French was even harder. For some reason, they did not employ even one Han character!

~

Soon, we moved to a larger apartment in the Pension de Famille in East Paris. My bedroom was large but dark. One of the things I remember most vividly was the bed—it was so large I could sleep horizontally, which was quite a change from my simple bed at home.

Siqui occupied the room next door and was quite busy with school and his friends. He also had learned to speak French, so he enjoyed the community much more than I did. Also, he was ten years older, so our interests were different.

He bought me a few things to keep me busy: a soccer ball to play with, a brush pen to write with, and some old Chinese books to learn about history, courage, and personal values. Since my French was so weak, I was reluctant to play outside with the neighborhood kids. I sat alone in my room for hours at a time, trying to release my sense of longing for home. I would bounce a soccer ball against the wall. Every so often, Siqui would stop by my room to say, "Stop, Little Brother, your noise is driving me crazy!"

I was also frustrated with my first attempts at playing the violin. I had no idea the instrument was so challenging to master and required diligent attention to detail. Slowly I learned the left hand on the strings made the musical notes, and the right hand held the bow and controlled the rhythm. Then there was the matter of shoulder placement; the sound varied greatly depending upon where you place the instrument. I was frustrated with my lack of progress.

Chapter 6.

My First Composition

我的第一个作品

Tragic Chinese hero, Xiang Yu, (ce-ange-enu), the subject of 12-year-old Ma's first composition.

Siqui again took the initiative to identify a more advanced violin teacher. Madame Adrienne was witty, charming, and dedicated. She immediately recognized my potential and insisted I practice three hours a day. I could feel the progress; I was now quite passionate about my music.

~

Six months later, Siqui thought it would be worthwhile for me to live with a French family while I studied. My landlord, who had a big red nose, was also an excellent French teacher. She would only speak French, so in two months I could speak French quite fluently. After I lived in the red-nosed landlord's home for about a year, and she gave me great lessons in the basics, we agreed it was time for me to receive formal music training at school.

We again changed teachers, this time to a female graduate of the prestigious Conservatoire de Paris. She was a skilled perfectionist and demanded timely attendance. I remember a day it was raining cats and dogs as I rode my bicycle to her home for class. When I arrived at her apartment, I was completely soaked and dripping. Everywhere I set foot, I left a pool of water on the floor. She looked confused and asked, "Ma, why don't you wear a raincoat?"

I did not have the heart to explain the truth. From when I was a child in my father's home, I wanted to be a fearless warrior to help create a united China. I believed that no matter the time of year (summer or winter) or weather (rain or sun), the most fearless warriors only wore two pieces of clothing. Right or wrong, I was always in good health; I never caught a cold or got sick.

Some months later, I decided to write a violin composition about a tragic Chinese hero by the name of Xiang Yu, who led a rebellion against the Qing Dynasty some two thousand years ago. I also composed a piece called "A Sadden Moon" based on a famous Chinese fairytale called *Sad Moon Fairy*.

The teacher was amazed at my ability to compose at 12 years of age. In 1925, after a brief audition, she had me placed in the advanced class at the Music Conservatory of Nancy, an affiliate of the highly respected Conservatoire de Paris.

As my skills improved, I realized Siqui and Siwu were thriving in their new Parisian environment. Siwu was taken by the intelligence and beauty of French women, and Siqui found the city an excellent place to utilize his business skills.

~

Occasionally, we would receive news from home. China seemed to go from one military crisis to another. Initially, I had no interest. My world was my violin.

Siqui and Siwu learned that Sun Yat-sen and his army, with help from nearby provinces, were engaged in a fierce military campaign with his former protégé Cheng, who refused to honor Sun Yat-sen's order to take control the North Territories by force to defer democratic reforms indefinitely. When Cheng retreated, Sun successfully re-occupied his home base in Guangdong. During the tensions, my father was again forced to leave home because of philosophical differences. This time he lived in Hong Kong for almost two years, and my mother was left to run the household, which she did without complaint.

~

Sun realized to maintain power and sublimate democratic reforms indefinitely, he needed to bolster his military strength beyond help from the nearby provinces. Initially, he went to the European community, who refused to get involved in internal Chinese affairs. Ultimately, Sun and his newly formed Nationalist Party of China received support from the new state of the Soviet Union, which provided funding, military advisors, and war materials.

About two years later, we received another letter from my father. He wrote that order had been restored in our homeland, and he was returning to Guangdong from Hong Kong with no job but with belief in the future. My father hoped to gain a well-paying position somewhere in Sun's government. Siqui was skeptical but said little. He realized our family might need financial support, and, as the oldest brother, it was primarily his responsibility.

Shortly after he returned, Sun was diagnosed with terminal gallbladder cancer. Ten weeks later, he was dead at the age of 59. So my father never got the job he had hoped for, and Sun never lived to see his party ultimately unify the country, but he did leave a political legacy known as the *Three Principles of the People* which exist to this day.

- Nationalism. Independence from foreign imperialists.
- Rights of the People. The Chinese version of democracy.
- People's Livelihood. Societal survival through socialism.

After Sun's death, his political heir, Chiang Kai-shek, tried to realize the dream of a reunited China by leading the Northern Expeditions. By 1927, Chiang brought the warring factions somewhat under control by alliance or submission.

Chapter 7.

Moving to Nancy

搬到南希

Young Ma lives and studies in the baroque city of Nancy, France.

Nancy, founded in 1050 A.D., was a beautiful, tranquil riverfront city knows for its art nouveau landmarks. I lived near the grand square, decorated with gilded wrought-iron gates and elaborate fountains, which I found to be a magnificent visual feast.

Most residents were kind Catholics, which I found to be very different from the hedonists of Paris. Located in northeast France, Nancy's weather was colder than Paris during the winter. Nevertheless, I maintained my two-clothes policy, even at temperatures of –20 Celsius. As a courtesy to other occupants, I never opened windows in the winter, but I also never turned on the heat; my landlord called my room a refrigerator.

Even though I was the youngest student in the class, the teachers were surprised that I could play complicated music notes so accurately.

My music classes were educational and fun! My teacher had a short, well-trimmed beard and loved to tell jokes and encouraged us to think of life as an incredible journey to the unknown. Since there were only 14 boys in the class, there was much personal attention and lots of jokes. I felt very comfortable and well-accepted and, most importantly, the teacher gave us the privilege to talk and make funny faces whenever we wished, so long as the work excelled.

One of my more memorable experiences was when the school's president, Monsieur Dubois, was invited to listen to each student's progress. I walked to the front of the classroom, placed my music on a stand, and played. He closed his eyes and listened. When I was finished, he asked an odd question.

"Ma, do you think you all Chinese people have good ears?" I could hear some students gasp. It was my first real encounter with bigotry, although I didn't know what to call it. I replied courteously, "Yes, I think so."

~

During my stay at the Conservatory of Nancy, I lived in the home of a very kind older woman who had a 31-year-old daughter. The daughter was an excellent pianist, so we often played recitals for friends in my landlord's home. In time, we developed a process which I would never forget. Since I was in charge of producing our compositions, I would go to the local music store and purchase all the music scorebooks, then fill them with notes and movements.

The Nancy school was a busy time for me, between music, studies, and the many friends I made. Despite having the best teacher in school, I knew many of my bow moves were incorrect. I felt the school emphasized the quantity of output over the quality of output.

As part of the final exams, the students had to perform in public, which I welcomed, although most of my classmates were in panic mode. I chose to play Paganini's *Violin Concerto No. 1*. I practiced many hours a day; I wanted my performance to be perfect.

When the winners were announced, I was awarded second prize. I was so disappointed that I could not even look at my teacher. I was now certain if I was to master my instrument, I had to leave Nancy, return to Paris, and tutor with the most exceptional teachers of the time.

Placing second was not good enough! I was a perfectionist.

Chapter 8.

Returning to Paris

返回巴黎

Conservatoire de Paris violin master Paul Oberdoerffer and his talented students (Ma upper right) share time at the Parisienne seaside

More committed than ever, I returned to Paris in early 1926. Siqui and I searched for the appropriate teacher and role model. Fortunately, a school friend introduced me to Paul Oberdoerffer, the highly respected violin master for the prestigious Opera National de Paris Orchestra.

I was told the school's entrance requirements were strict; only six out of every 100 applicants were selected for study, and there had never been a single Asian student.

I decided I would play a relatively new work, Lalo's *Symphonie Espagnole,* which had been introduced in Paris in 1875. I chose the piece because I wanted to demonstrate I was more than just an Asian impersonating a professionally trained classical violinist. I wanted the teachers to realize I was a serious student of symphonic evolution with a broad understanding of melodic invention and rhythmic flair.

His criticism was unfamiliar but insightful. "Ma, your musical expression is perfect, but you committed many technical errors."

Courteously, I challenged him. "Such as?"

Oberdoerffer saw disappointment and rage; he spoke softly, but clearly. "Your right-hand holds the bow incorrectly, and parts of your left fingers are placed incorrectly on the strings. As a result, your sound is less defined. When it comes to the violin, the difference between a virtuoso and a good musician is a collection of small but important details. The good news is that you are young; these mistakes can be easily corrected now."

I thought to myself, how much time have I wasted? I've spent three years in France, and this is the first time a teacher has identified these technical errors. Fortunately, Oberdoerffer agreed to become my teacher. Between lessons, I spent six hours a day practicing. I also studied the piano with Oberdoerffer's wife, who was a well-regarded classical pianist. With their help, I made significant improvements in both violin technic and musical expression.

About six months later, Oberdoerffer felt I was ready to apply for entrance to the prestigious Conservatoire de Paris. Since it opened in 1795, the staff and students included some of the most influential composers and violinists in music, such as Pierre Monsigny, `Etienne Mèhul, Pierre Ballot, and Pierre Rode.

I was excited, but not feeling particularly well. I was experiencing some pain in my neck, which created a loss of feeling in my hands. At first, I ignored it as a youthful discomfort. Thirty days later, I was having trouble playing; my hands felt weak. The doctors identified a large cyst on my neck that was pressing against my nerves. Instead of surgery, he suggested I stop playing and spend time in the seaside town of Berck sur Mer because "continued exposure to fresh salt air was the best natural cure for a cyst, rather than a dangerous surgery."

In March of 1927, Siqui, who had graduated from university, and I traveled about 200 miles from Paris to Berck by train. The city had a long shoreline and pristine wide sandy beaches, unlike anything I'd ever seen in China. We noticed many patients were recuperating from one illness or another, riding horses and lying on carriages, soaking in the clear air and the bright sunshine.

My handsome brother and I (now 16) made friends quite quickly, especially with the girls. Eventually, we had a circle of ten friends that did everything together—swim, play ball, sunbathe, and watch music shows. I could see the cyst starting to shrink.

Summer arrived. Suddenly the town was filled with tourists, all the hotels were full, and thousands of people gathered in the bright sunshine on the white sandy beaches. My imagination grew during these days. I felt as though I were on an extended vacation rather than recuperating from an illness. The thick leaves were making beautiful music as they swayed in seas breezes and bright summer sunshine. I thought to myself, one day, I will create a musical composition that will remind me of these joyful moments.

Soon, summer was over, and everything changed. The tourists gradually disappeared. Siqui realized my recuperation was going well, and he knew it was time for him to return to China to help support our family. Suddenly, I was all alone in a vast hotel filled with unoccupied rooms, a gigantic empty hall, and a closed billiards room. I felt like a hermit.

Things went from bad to worse. Autumn and winter came; the wide beaches were transformed into a dark, barren desert with cold northern winds. I felt abandoned, but I knew I had no choice but to deal with my loneliness if I was ever going to play the violin again. I decided to turn my feelings of isolation into a search for self-discovery. Suddenly, I saw the raw beauty as the northern winter wind make the beach sand swirl, and the fishy smell of seawater cleared my nostrils. As the sun set on the edge of the far seas, I imagined skies filled with rainbow-colored clouds. Nature's continuing show brought me a calmness that is hard to describe in words.

To spend my time productively, I went downstairs to the hall and practiced the piano and read books, mostly about great composers like Bach, Mozart, Liszt, and Chopin. The more I explored the piano's range of notes, the more I learned about melody. Piano music —especially that of the great French musicians like Debussy and Ravel—increased my understanding of multi-part homophony, where one melody predominates, and the accompanying parts are simple chords.

Tuesday, December 27, 1927, was my last day in Berck. It was depressingly snowy, windy, and cold. While I had not played the violin for some time, I left pleased with my growth as a musician. And the cyst on my neck was completely healed.

Chapter 9.

Siqui Returns Home

思齐回家

(left to right) Ma's older brothers, Siqui and Siwu, in Paris.

Siqui asked Siwu to join him on the long trip home, since they both had graduated.

"Why?" asked Siwu, who had fallen madly in love with a young Frenchwoman from a well-to-do family that happened to be his landlord's daughter.

"From the letters, I believe our parents may need financial support," replied Siqui, who had a good business sense. During school, Siqui discovered that the French loved Chinese handmade embroidered artwork, and there were numerous skilled Chinese women without jobs. So, he and two relatives in China formed a company to export the embroidery made by village women. Everybody won; Siqui and his partners earned lots of cash, local women had well-paying jobs, and the French bought beautiful handmade goods unavailable nowhere else. But Siqui realized that for the business to grow, he needed additional help.

"For how long?" asked Siwu. "I'm not certain," said Siqui.

Siwu paused. "I love my parents, but I do not want to lose my Lenore. Respectfully, I must decline."

~

A few days later, Siqui approached me.

"Ma, please come back to China and help me." I was shocked. "Help you do what?"

My brother replied sincerely, "I need help with the business."

"I don't understand. You already have two relatives helping you. And Siwu is better suited."

"Siwu is in love and wishes to remain in Paris. I cannot deny him that. As for the other relatives, their abilities are limited; they can only work in the villages buying embroidery arts to fill orders. I need someone like you who can speak French fluently to work with my French-speaking customers in Guangzhou and Shanghai. Adding a few large orders a year will be good enough; I am so busy managing the business, I don't have the extra time to do that. If you would come and help, I will be at ease knowing you can negotiate in French. That way, we will always be treated fairly, and our business will grow even bigger."

"I don't know anything about business, " I replied. "I only know how to play the violin."

Siqui's eyes moistened, "You're my close brother. I love you. You are the only one I can completely trust, and you'll be able to ensure our other relatives are not cheating us."

I felt terrible. I was torn. I wanted to help Siqui—he had done so much for me—but not at the cost of giving up my violin studies. "I am deeply sorry, Siqui, but I cannot."

It would be the first and only time I ever refused my oldest brother, whom I greatly respected. Siqui understood my struggle. "Ma, I'm not asking you to give up the violin; you can still play at leisure or nighttime. Remember, I gave you your first violin; I believe in your great gift."

~

"Let me sleep on it," I replied, unable to again say no. That night, I tossed in bed; I was deeply conflicted. Did I love my brother or my music more? What was the right choice for our family and for me?

The more I tossed, the more anxious I became. The sounds of the street seemed relentless, louder than ever. Finally, I rose and paced the room. The light of the full moon streamed through my bedroom. I picked up my violin and began to play Franz Schubert's *Serenade* to calm my nerves, to relieve my pain and anxiety. When the music stopped, I was at peace. I released a long, heavy sigh and turned to get back in bed; Siqui stood in the doorway. He applauded softly.

"Ma, that was outstanding; your music and technique touched my soul. I realize it would be wrong to take your music away from you. Stay and complete your studies. Don't stop halfway."

I didn't know how to respond. My brother was so kind-hearted and sincere; I could feel the love. I jumped up and firmly embraced Siqui as the tears rolled down my face, "I love you very much, dear brother."

Siqui replied, "I have only one request. I'd like you to talk to Siwu. He also understands your gift; he wants you to succeed. Tell him about our family's difficult financial situation, and give him my advice; if Siwu honestly loves that girl, as you love your music, he should marry her and bring her home to China. I know I can rely on him to be my helper. As the oldest, I know I must lift the heavy financial burdens from our aging parents and our less fortunate other brothers and sisters. But, as the next oldest, Siwu also has some responsibility to share this burden."

I nodded. "I promise to do my very best."

Siqui continued, "As for you, I'm convinced the world will one day feel your determination, see your natural talent, and hear your music."

As we embraced, I again realized the importance of family and respect in my culture. I was proud to be Chinese. Siqui could have easily pursued his doctorate in France and became a wealthy businessman, but for the sake of our family's honor, he sacrificed his ambitions and his future.

Chapter 10.

Learning from a Master

向大师学习

Ma's highly respected violin teacher, Jules Boucherit.

After Breck, I continued my studies at the Conservatoire de Paris. My new teacher was the highly respected Jules Boucherit, to whom the school assigned its most gifted students. I was proud of my selection and wrote home to tell my parents.

I quickly discovered Boucherit was considered a violin pedagogue, a word with no equivalent in Chinese. Boucherit was a student of teaching. He spent many hours refining his teaching process based on the knowledge and skills of classical violin masters. He believed having a process based in history provided clarity and authenticity to his teaching. At the same time, he considered that part of his job was to remain flexible. He knew the best students also responded best to practical new ideas designed for their particular strengths. And he knew that efficient learning also incorporated the social, political, and cultural contexts of each student. He never wanted to delay the progress of his students inadvertently.

~

I was the first Asian student in the school's history. I would be less than honest if I didn't say I felt intimidated by Boucherit and my all-white European counterparts.

After my first solo performance, he took me aside and explained in clear, straightforward language, "Ma, you must be careful with your artistry. Many musicians seeking fame think they should disregard the past and only chase new things. They are wrong; history teaches us we are not wise to cut ourselves off from the soul of the past."

I listened but did not fully grasp the abstract concept. Boucherit sensed my hesitation; he took a particular interest in me as a person and as an artist. One Sunday, Boucherit decided to take me to the Louvre to show me how great artists blend historic technique with new ideas to create art that is distinctly theirs.

We stood in front of the painting of a cow by Rembrandt. He said, "See the beauty?"

I shrugged. "It's a cow."

"Yes and no," he replied. "True, this is a painting about the muscles and bones of a cow. In that sense, it is no different than a boring, well-crafted anatomical painting in a hospital." He paused and moved his hands gracefully around the lines of the painting. "But this is an outstanding, elegant piece of art. Feel the flow. That is the mark of a great artist: they can turn a common, simple subject into a passionate, moving work."

As we sat on the bench outside the museum, he offered thoughts on the elegance of simplicity. "Do you know how many syllables are in Beethoven's Symphony No. 5?"

"I'm not sure," I replied.

"Just seven, and they are assigned to the notes of a scale so the musician can hear the pitches of a piece of music the first time he sees and hears a composition. Most musicians understand the concept of seven syllables, but the great musician has the genius to adjust their use to what pleases him. That is how great composition is born. Do you realize the first chapter of Beethoven's Symphony No. 5 was established with the use of only two syllables?"

Boucherit paused and smiled. "And Brahms often used only bottom sounds as melody, employing syllables at an extreme minimum."

That evening, I went home and listened to Beethoven and Brahms for hours. I made myself a promise: never forget Boucherit's message that "simplicity is beauty."

On another Sunday, Boucherit discussed my musical technique in unlikely terms. He told me my artistic technique was the unlikely combination of the romantic poet Lord Byron and the cerebral philosopher Friedrich Nietzsche.

"Ma," he said, "like Byron, your music has an unmistakable spirit of beauty, but your notes conjure the passion of Nietzsche. They whip you into a frenzy which strikes deep into one's soul. I have heard and taught many gifted students, but I am not sure any have ever combined history and technique quite that way. Barring the unforeseen, your country will one day be proud of your legacy."

As a 15-year-old, I was in awe of Boucherit's prediction. At that moment, I also had no knowledge of how history would shape the next 62 years.

Chapter 11.

Playing My Way Home

玩回家的路

Ma returns to China on the super-lux Andre Lebon steamship.

Siqui's letters from home contained little detail of the current difficulties, but I felt compelled to go home and see what I could do to help. On February 7, 1929, I boarded the Andre Lebon in Marseille Harbor with a third-class ticket, one change of clothes, and a few dollars in my pocket.

Initially, I was excited as the big ship sailed smoothly on the calm waters of the Mediterranean Sea. The sky and seawater were an endless blue that stretched forever. As I sat in my cabin, the constant blue followed by the black night made me feel dull and lifeless. I decided to play my violin as a way to escape the boredom. Hearing my notes could transport me to another place and time. One day while I was playing, there was a sudden knock on the cabin door. To my surprise, the smiling captain stood in the doorway. "Hi, young man, I've heard about you." He put his arm around me, with four gold stripes on his sleeve. "Can I make a deal with you?"

"What deal?" I was confused. He did not have any merchandise on the ship.

"Okay, it is like this. Our ship will take one month and five days to reach Shanghai. During such a long journey, we have to entertain our first-class guests. We frequently have evening parties. If you're willing to play at the parties, all your meals on the trip will be on us."

"Okay!" I responded, imagining the happy faces on the guests and my stomach full of delicacies like lobsters and steaks.

After the captain left, my Chinese roommate patted me on the shoulder. "Congratulations on such a great deal."

I stared. "I didn't spend years studying the violin to pay for meals." But free food was free food, and it was delicious! So I performed many of the popular classics almost every night.

I thought of these live performances as rehearsals for what would someday be a real concert tour.

~

I didn't know what to expect when I got off the boat in Shanghai. I hadn't been home in six years. I missed my homeland, my parents, and my brothers and sisters, especially my oldest brother Siqui, who had returned home two years earlier. I imagined a joyfully blessed, peaceful China, and a comfortable, happy family. The reality was something else. Shanghai had not yet recovered from the massacres two years ago when Chiang Kai-shek purged the Chinese Communist members. The bloody event was still fresh in people's minds. Shanghai was silent, dull, and still. Hours later, I stepped through the front gate of my home, anxious to see my parents and siblings. The family swarmed around, and we embraced. The tears flowed freely. My mother wiped away her tears and stood in front of me, staring with pleasure. She could not believe her naughty little boy had turned into such a handsome young man. She embraced me again as she whispered in my ear, "I have dreamt of this moment for six years. Now that you are standing here, it feels like a dream." She slowly stroked my head and softly cried out my nickname, "My Ai! my Ai!"

My mother's appearance had not changed very much, but my father was a different matter. He looked sad; he had deep wrinkles in his face and looked much older than he had six years ago. He also walked slowly and insecurely. When I hugged him, he felt frail. He was no longer the sturdy disciplinarian I feared growing up.

The one most changed was my oldest brother, Siqui. In the two years since we parted at Breck, Siqui's confident, scholarly demeanor had changed. He talked about business nonstop from the moment I arrived; he had been completely transformed into a merchant seeking profits whenever and wherever he could.

His interest in world matters had disappeared, and he had no interest in discussing my experiences, violin, or lessons. He no longer even had a violin. And he looked like another person. He had traded in his neat suit, shirt and tie, and leather shoes for a long, embroidered gown. His neatly combed, shiny hair was now long strips of dark black hair tied in the back of his head.

~

While I was home, I thought about using my violin skills and growing reputation to help my parents. I knew that during the early twentieth century, many world-renowned violinists, including Fritz Kreisler, Jascha Heifetz, Jacques Thibaud, and Szymon Goldberg, had performed in China in front of large audiences. They provided rare opportunities for the Chinese to appreciate the beauty of the violin, which was generally unknown in China.

I decided I would start a modest tour and hope for the best. My father introduced me to various government officials who saw my tour as a means of instilling pride in the new Chinese Republic. They had become aware of my talents, and they and the government saw my tour as a way of telling the Chinese people that we have a violinist who can play as well as the first-rate foreign violinists. The fact that I was young and considered handsome by most women did not hurt my appeal.

Unlike father, I was not the least interested in politics; I didn't care if the government saw me as a propaganda instrument. My only interest was to bring world-class violin music to the Chinese masses.

My first concert in Guangzhou was sold out; we went on to perform more concerts that winter in many of China's largest cities, including Hong Kong, Nanjing, and Shanghai. The remarks of the Chinese press were kind. In Hong Kong, they wrote, "There is now a yellow skin man with black eyeballs who has become China's violin prodigy." In Shanghai, an influential critic wrote, "Ma Sicong's recent performance brought the audience to new levels of excitement and tranquility. Our whiz kid (I was only 18) is mesmerizing and uplifting."

After reading the reviews, I thought about the societal importance of my work. Since the fall of the Qing, Western culture had significantly influenced our new Chinese society. Unintentionally, my music created a new musical realm where Western musical elements and Eastern art forms intersected. I was not only helping to build a foundation for classical Chinese music, but I was also restoring pride to the citizens of our glorious civilization.

While the praise and accomplishments were flattering, the most important thing to me was that these first tours allowed me to earn some money to give my parents. While he didn't say much, I think Siqui was proud of my accomplishments; he knew his sacrifices were not in vain.

~

I planned to return to Paris after the tours to master the art of composition. But in January 1930, I was offered the position of the first violinist for the orchestra of the Dramatic Arts in Guangzhou.

So I decided to stay a bit longer. Rather quickly, I noticed two things: my performances sold out quickly, and they attracted many beautiful women who listened, smiled, and swooned. They not only liked my music, but they also liked my looks!

One evening, I was introduced to an elegant young girl, Guo Ziyu (*gau-se-yu*), with a kind smile. We started seeing each other. I remember taking walks in the park and serenading her with my music. She loved it. Soon, I introduced her to my parents. My entire family took an immediate liking. My mother whispered, "She is kind and gentle; she makes a good girlfriend, and then who knows?" I was over the moon.

Things did not work out as I expected. When I met her parents, they were very friendly. But in the course of that first evening, her father learned that, despite my bilingual sophistication and European musical adventures, I was still the son of peasants who had a revolutionary father. I was neither wealthy nor privileged. But Guo agreed to rendezvous in Paris when the time was right.

~

It was now time to leave my troubled China, my aging parents, my beloved siblings, and my unselfish older brother. Siqui accompanied me to the harbor to board the Andre Lebron to Marseille, where we would then make our way to Paris.

Before boarding, Siqui took out a stack of money from his white and blue gown and handed it to me. "Little Brother, Paris is expensive, as are your lessons. This should help ease the burden. I know you have no idea how to make money."

Siqui took out a second stack. "This is for Siwu. Tell him his family needs him at home. If he loves that woman so much, tell him to use this money to marry her, and then bring his new wife home to live with our family—Mother and Father will not live forever." I could feel the urgency in Siqui's words.

We hugged one last time on the dock. It was a bittersweet moment I would remember the rest of my life.

~

Shortly after I returned to Paris, I met with Siwu, gave him the money for his marriage dowry, and passed on Siqui's request that the couple return to China once married. He was appreciative but remained hesitant.

Not long after that, Siwu asked for his girlfriend's hand in marriage. They married in France, Siwu renamed her Zhuge, and they moved to Shanghai which, at the time, was the most cosmopolitan large city in China with an international melting pot of Germans, Russians, and British, among others. Siwu felt his wife was far too sophisticated for his little hometown of Haifeng. My brother became a respected French teacher at Shanghai Foreign College.

They bought a charming house in a quiet, wooded section of town. They had no children, just two pets they adored—a dog and cat—and a series of regular routines. Every evening after dinner, they would get appropriately dressed and take the dog for a walk along the quiet streets. Zhuge, who insisted on wearing high heels in public, would click loudly on the sidewalks in the silent night air. On Saturdays, they would play poker with each other.

Zhuge, while warm and friendly, did not like to socialize outside of family members. Siwu was her whole world. She loved being my brother's wife and excelled at making loaves of fresh-baked bread, fluffy biscuits filled with sweet and salty aromas, and classic French treats like croissants and brioche. My sister-in-law was also quite the tailor. She made Siwu suits and overcoats; her hand-woven pillows and tapestries dotted sofas and chairs throughout the house.

In many ways, they were the perfect couple—admittedly, from another time. I cannot even remember a time when they raised their voice to each other. Every morning, Zhuge would kiss Siwu goodbye before he left for work, then spend her day cleaning, shopping, and preparing a delicious dinner for Siwu.

Our older brother, Siqui, used to tell Mother, "Siwu and Zhuge are like a bottle of fine French wine: mature and filled with many pleasing sensations." I always thought Siqui's description, while well-intended, was a bit odd. But I said nothing; after all, he was my older brother!

Chapter 12.

Learning Composition

学习作曲

Albert Binenbaum taught Ma how to be a world-class composer

With financial support from the Guangdong regional government, I returned to France in 1931 to study composition at the Conservatoire de Paris. The question was, with whom?

Like many young artists, I had insecurities. Were my notes too shallow and my technique ordinary? Would my compositions ever be good enough?

I met with my former teacher, violin master Oberdoerffer. He not only understood my insecurities, but he also had a solution. "The traditional rules governing the development of composition are not suitable for your gifts. You need a professor who is freer and bolder. I've considered several Conservatoire professors, including the famed Albert Roussel. But I think my friend Albert Binenbaum is the best choice for you."

Binenbaum was a Turkish composer of Jewish descent, who served as musical director in Regensburg, Hamburg, and Berlin. He arrived at the Conservatoire about five years before me. Binenbaum never achieved the fame he deserved. However, he would go on to play a significant role in the enduring nature of the 57 symphonies I would write during my lifetime.

~

Oberdoerffer pointed to a large photo of Binenbaum on the wall and said, "To play his quartet, I spent nearly three months in practice! It is such a deep and hard composition." Oberdoerffer picked up his violin and played a few stanzas of Binenbaum's work. I was impressed; the melody was so peculiarly different and profoundly intense.

We first met at Oberdoerffer's home. Binenbaum's head was even more prominent than in his photo—he had a broad and high tilted forehead on a kind, skinny face. We chatted a little bit, and then he gave me a time to start my first class. His teaching method appeared to contain contradictions. "Learning must be disciplined to make your compositions free." Then he gave me an extensive, diverse collection of exercises for homework.

I remember showing him my first assigned work, a short piece. I was nervous; Binenbaum was not known for compliments. "It has a good effect, but overall it's not quite good enough" His praise, such as it was, heightened my spirits and caused me to work even harder. I can still hear the sound of car horns drifting through my window as the clock passed midnight in the bustling Paris night.

On weekends, I would ride the train for a half hour or more to Binenbaum's country home in the woods. Binenbaum would visit my rehearsal room and examine every note of my existing homework assignments. He'd use a sharp pencil to correct an error, then put the used pencil into his pocket. At the end of class, his pocket would be full of pencils. Then he'd give me my next assignments and would return with a new bundle of pencils at my next class. He used to laugh, "When I have fewer pencils in my pocket, we will both know you have made sufficient progress."

He was like a wise old friend who often identified the strengths and weaknesses of well-known works of art.

"Ma," he would say, "I am not trying to persuade you to accept my opinion; I merely want you to know that I have one.

"You have the God-given talent to be a great musician. But part of becoming a great artist is to understand the thinking of other great artists so that you can shape your work in the way you find most pleasing." I soon became deeply involved in studying great paintings, listening to beautiful music, and reading literary masterpieces to fuel my self-improvement as an artist and composer.

Binenbaum and I frequented many of Paris's museums. Our favorite place was the Louvre. The museum housed an abundance of outstanding artwork, from the Italian Renaissance's great masters to France's Fauvism favorites. One day, we sat on the bench in front of da Vinci's *Mona Lisa*. The feeling was intoxicating. In time, Binenbaum taught me to appreciate the multiple dimensions weaved into many of the great classical and newer works. Although, in all honesty, I never understood abstract artwork and found they didn't provide any musical inspiration.

~

In our leisure time together, Binenbaum taught me another valuable life lesson: great artists are never afraid to change. "There was nothing more frightening for the true artists than to stop growing," he said. "Part of Picasso's genius was his willingness to expose the immature side of his art, then have the audacity to create another work with an unimagined level of maturity."

Years later, I remember discussing the evolution of artistic maturity with my good friend, the great Chinese painter Qi Baish, when he was 93. "Ma," he said, "my paintings had progressed nicely from my 80s, when they were so innocent and naïve." [1]

~

Thanks to Binebaum, when I played Bach, the modesty and simplicity of Rembrandt's paintings would come to mind. When I played Mendelssohn, I visualized *The Birth of Venus* by Sandro Botticelli at the Uffizi Gallery, where Venus gradually emerges from blue sea water fully-grown, fresh, soft, and tranquil.

Once Binenbaum paid me the ultimate compliment. He said an early composition was imbued with the gracefulness of the French composer Claude Debussy's *La fille aux cheveux de lin* ("The girl with the flaxen hair").

The more I studied in Paris, the more I realized artistic development in my homeland lacked the sophistication of Europe. Chinese Dynasty arts contained several elements of grandeur. The Sixth Dynasty stone carvings and sculptures were solemn, intelligent, full of creative spirit and youthful energy. Meanwhile, Tang paintings were grand but too neat, and the Song Dynasty was weak, lacking vitality and creativity.

~

Finally, Binenbaum thought it was time for me to learn Counterpoint: the mediation of two or more musical lines into an unexpected, yet meaningful and pleasing whole. Before we began lessons, we strolled through his rose garden. He asked, "Do you like my garden?"

"I have never seen so many different colors and fragrances, and never experienced such beauty in one place," I replied.

He smiled. "My young friend, you now understand the concept of counterpoint. It is your job to capture the technique before you in your works." In time, I learned how to research the counterpoint secrets of structure, harmony, and technique of many great

---

[1] While Qi Baishi is not a household name in America, one of his paintings recently sold for $61 million at a Chinese auction.

musicians, including Beethoven, Schubert, Mendelssohn, Brahms, Schumann, and Chopin.

~

Although he could have all that life had to offer, Binenbaum lived the simple life of a vegetarian and prided himself on the fact that he never got sick, never even had a fever. I complimented him on his austere regimen but told him I had no plans to do likewise. "I do not see any relationship between diet and great composition!"

He replied simply and humbly. "Each man must do as he believes, so be it."

Chapter 13.

My First China Tours

我的第一次中国之旅

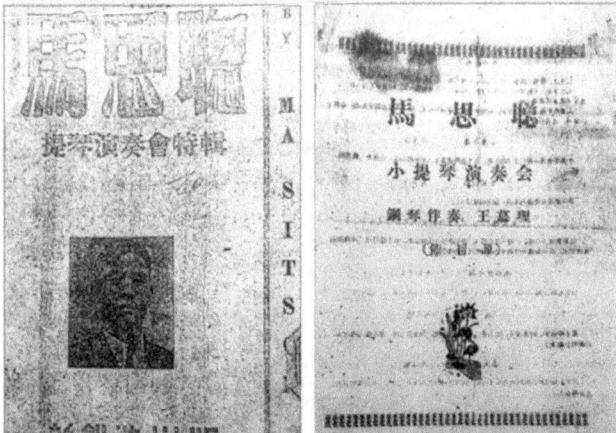

Ma toured China, Hong Kong, Taipei, and Shanghai in 1931-32.

When I returned from Paris the second time in 1931, I realized my life would never be the same.

I had grown up in postwar Paris during *Les années folles* (the crazy years), when the city re-established itself as a worldwide leader in art, music, and literature. And I had the good fortune to be exposed firsthand to great artists like Picasso, Dali, Hemingway, and Joyce. I was intoxicated by their search for artistic truth, their vigorous attention to detail, and their quest for innovation, while deeply concerned with their self-destructive appetite for the good life. The China I came home to was a very different place. In essence, no Chinese cities had a reputation for artistic or musical excellence, and traditional Chinese moral values were at odds with everything Parisian. Chinese music education lagged far behind the Western standards I had come to accept as the norm.

So, I made a decision—I would become my country's spokesperson for the beauty of Western classical music. As I think back, my choice at the age of 20 to accept such responsibility was both heroic and naive!

~

With the support of government officials, gathered through my father's political connections, I received the funds and promotional support to fund and recruit the first all-Chinese classical orchestra in my Guangzhou hometown. I quickly discovered there was an acute shortage of talented twentieth century musicians, so I performed a series of concerts in Nanking, Shanghai, Hong Kong, and Guangzhou to increase awareness of the orchestra, recruit musical candidates, and earn money for my family and me.

The following spring, I co-founded the first private music school in China, the Guangzhou Conservatory of Music, modeled after the Conservatoire in Paris. My goal was to ensure my students received the same quality musical education I had received in Europe, but there was no Binenbaum, Oberdoerffer, or Boucherit to teach. So initially, I had to wear many hats, in addition to being president. I taught violin, music theory, ear training, and piano, and I served as concertmaster and conductor of the orchestra and choruses at my conservatory, and I even became a lecturer at Nanking Central University, again another first for someone only 23 years old.

~

When I started to pursue composing allegro music, I tried a string quarter minor for the first time. I sent the sheet music from Guangzhou to Binenbaum for his opinion. He replied, "Your technique is first-rate, your music is solemn, and you are on the correct pass. However, there are many repetitions without perforation; they are also weak in harmony and have a lack of character."

Painful as the critique was, I realized Binenbaum was urging me to connect music with real life, something I had not accomplished to date. At the time, I was living in the Lake Xuanwu *(zen-woo)* area, a famous South China resort destination in Nanking. One sunny afternoon, I watched the smooth waters of Xuanwu Lake as I recalled the poem "Ode to a Nightingale" by John Keats. As I stood on the deck, passing ships headed for the Mediterranean Sea. The experience was mesmerizing; I decide to combine my sensory experiences into a full-length melody, *Piano Trio in B major.*

In the spring, I returned to the lake to enjoy the aroma of new grasses, flowers, and the warble of birds singing. I combined all those joyful elements—happiness, youth, and sunshine—in another new composition, *Violin sonata No. 1 in G major*, which to this day is one of my personal favorites.

In Shanghai and Nanking, I performed the *Sonata in G major* for the first time, with the critically acclaimed pianist Harry Ore in Guangzhou. The encores were so enthusiastic that Harry and I played several unplanned pieces as a thank you. That was also the evening I realized that the performing artist loves audience recognition, even though they may be unwilling to admit such to their peers.

The day after the concert, the prestigious *Hong Kong South China Morning Post* wrote in Chinese, English, and French.

"Sitson Ma, a young man with an attractive personality, and a modest, competent manner, gave a recital at the Helena May Institute on Monday evening, with the assistance of Harry Ore at the piano.

"Sitson studied at the well-regarded Paris Conservatoire and now is engaging in teaching music at the Central University, Nanking. I was told that Ma was a composer with merit, with some considerable works already accomplished. Since hearing the musicality of his violin, I am eager to make acquaintance with all his compositions.

"It was a pleasant shock to find myself swept by this young man's ability to run the gamut of emotion from gracious appreciation to unaccustomed enthusiasm. Ma's performance was as good as I have heard in many years of concert-going, and far in advance of most."

The concert's favorable newspaper reviews caught the attention of the country's rulers, the Kuomintang Party of China. Soon, I was invited to become a member of the national government's music committee. I was reluctant at first because, unlike my father, I wanted no part of politics, upheavals, and revolutions. But my father convinced me that in modern China, I could achieve my goals, help the country achieve its musical destiny, and still remain free from politics.

~

Despite my growing success, my parents didn't know anything about western trends in classical music. But, as parents, they remained proudly interested in my career. Whenever I held a concert within traveling distance of home, my mother would attend, rain or shine, summer or winter. Father was less present because of his need to attended political meetings in unknown destinations that he never discussed.

I recall vividly that my mother always arrived before the concert began and never was late. Her neatly combed hair was and made into a bun in the back of her head. Unlike many of the women of the time, she refused to cut her hair. Mother also wore her best clothes, which could best be described as those of a conservative old Chinese lady.

Her arrival at my concerts attracted attention, but nobody ever knew this mystery lady was my mother. They simply knew her age and apparel did not fit the circumstances. The audience, comprised mostly of attractive, well-groomed, young, modern-dressed women who swooned with excitement, wondered why this old-fashioned lady chose to attend a young virtuoso's violin concert rather than a Peking or Canton opera attended by senior citizens.

When the concert began, my mother sat silent, straight, and expressionless from beginning to the end, listening intently. She never exchanged words with any of my brothers and sisters who accompanied her. When the recital was over and the audience applauded, my mother smiled and clapped. Nobody ever knew how much she enjoyed my music. When asked which piece she loved the most, Mother always said, "I love them all."

Until her death, my mother was my most faithful audience.

Chapter 14.

Meeting Muli

遇到慕理

Ma, at the age of 21, meets the love of his life, Wang Muli

One day, I was in my office at the Guangzhou Conservatory of Music when a skinny young man holding a violin and a registration form entered.

He was four years older than I but he had a fire in his eyes. "Play a piece," I requested. After he finished, I said

"Your violin training is excellent. If you like, you can join my advanced class, and I'll teach you directly."

"Mr. Ma, how many people are in the advanced class?"

"Now there are three. Adding you, we will have four."

One week later, one of my students, Wang Heng (*hung*) came with a youngster who had some training with Wang. I took a look at the registration form: a high school student named Wang Youji (*yo-chi*) . He said he wanted to learn cello. "Wang Heng, is this your younger brother?"

"Yes, I explained to him the great improvements I had made with the violin. My brother insisted he wants to come to the school to further his cello skills."

"Cello is another class I teach, and I will assign you to that class."

~

A week later, Wang Heng brought a fashionable young lady wearing glasses, vivid red lipstick, a purple qipao with small flower decoration, and modern white high heels. I decided to crack a joke. "My friend, Wang, you bring another one! I think the school ought to award you with a scholarship for bringing us so many new students."

"This is my younger sister," he said.

The young lady interrupted her brother and smiled a slight smile. "Let me introduce myself. My name is Wang Muli *(moulie)* I want to learn the piano."

I cracked another joke. "Wang Heng, how many brothers and sisters do you have?

Muli glared; she did not find my joke funny. It was the first of many times that I would experience the fire of determination in her eyes.

"I have one younger brother and two younger sisters," replied Wang Heng.

"Next time, simply bring them all over." "He cannot do that," said Muli.

"Why?"

"My family has separated us into two groups," said Muli, who explained in one big breath. "I am the oldest girl, and my big brother Heng and younger brother Youji are one group. We love music. My mother, another younger brother, and two younger sisters are different; they love medicine because mother is a medical doctor."

Wang Heng laughed. "My sister Muli is the queen of my family." I looked at the registration form—she was just two years older than me but exuded self-confidence.

Not knowing what to expect, I looked at Muli, "Miss Wang, can you play something?"

Muli was not very good. I struggled to find a proper response. She came to my rescue. "Professor, I know I don't play well, but I will work hard to improve. I need a good teacher like you." I hesitated. I didn't want to waste my time, but Wang Heng pleaded, "Professor Ma, I promise you, my sister will work very hard."

"Alright, I will start a beginner's class for you today."

Wang Heng and his sister Wang Muli offered me many thanks. Wang Muli became the only student in my so-called beginners' class. She was, for all intents and purposes, my private student.

~

After a few lessons, I realized Muli was very intelligent and quick to learn, but her musical technique needed a great deal of improvement. Professionally, she held my music talent in high regard, and followed my instructions precisely, without hesitation. Soon, her musical sensitivity showed surprising improvement. While she never said anything, she told me later she found me a bit immature and naïve, but sincere and honest.

She was stubborn and fearless on matters relating to social behavior. In that regard, she was more like the self-confident Western women I had met in Paris. She was never ashamed to say Chinese women were too passive, too beholden to men, and lacked ideas of their own.

Muli's stubbornness led to arguments over inconsequential matters that, if allowed to persist, would exhaust my creative sensitivities. Besides, she was a passionate and articulate debater; it was usually more comfortable for me to acquiesce on non-musical issues. As I learned later in the United States, "The pain was not worth the gain."

~

Every one of my mentors reinforced the idea that a musical artist had to have broad views of life, such as with nature, arts, literature, and poetry. As Muli's mentor, it was my obligation to pass along the same philosophical view. So, in our leisure times, we visited many of Guangzhou city's cultural and scenic spots, including the Canton Tower, Temple of the Six Trees, Pearl River, and White Cloud Mountain.

One day, we spent the whole day at the Guangdong Museum, which housed nearly one thousand pictures of the city's development on the first floor, as well as thousands of rare artifacts from the Sui to Qing dynasties (4000 BC to 589 AD) on the other levels.

Muli had many questions, which I patiently answered in detail. "My goodness Professor Ma," she said. "How can you know so much!" Muli respected her young professor even more.

I laughed. "I love history, and I love to read. Don't forget; I was also once a museum curator."

The affection in her eyes warmed my heart. I was in love.

~

One day, Muli suggested we visit the newly established Guangzhou Museum in Yuexiu *(ti-cho)* Park. It was a beautiful spring day, and the multi-colored roses were in full bloom; their aromas were overwhelming. Suddenly, a soft breeze brought a small cluster of songbirds to rest on the soft petals. "This place is so beautiful," I said.

"I know," replied Muli.

"You have been here before with your family?" I asked. "No, with my fiancé."

I was jealous and depressed at the thought Muli belonged to another. "Oh! I didn't realize you are engaged."

"*Was* engaged," said Muli, with a hint of defiance. "I will not make that mistake again."

Soon, Muli and I decided to live together. She took care of our private life, and I concentrated on my compositions and career. Muli redecorated our first apartment in Guangzhou with simple, old furniture redesigned to look elegant and beautiful, and she filled every room with happy karma using fresh flowers, green plants, and an endless variety of incense aromas.

Chapter. 15.

My Little Family Secret

我的小家庭秘密

Ma reveals a fact of his life for the first time.

For various reasons, my mother never liked my choice of Wang Muli as a life partner, much less as my wife. So, *we never married*—despite what all the history books say!

For one thing, my mother thought of us as a prominent Chinese family. My father was a scholar under the Qing dynasty, and when China became a republic in the 1920s, his political influence grew. She was proud of the fact that he was named Finance Minister of Canton province, and only one of a handful of Chinese families who could afford to send three kids to study in France at the same time. Mother felt Muli's father was a common man with no particular stature, breeding, or political influence.

My mother was also never sure Muli loved me, the person; she believed Muli was more attracted to my reputation as a musical icon. Mother thought, with all her heart, that Muli had used her strong personality to trick me into our relationship, and that I was too gentle and kind to admit I'd made a mistake.

Disagreement between our mothers festered for decades. I remember Muli's mother making the point at a family gathering, "If your son truly loves my daughter, they should have a formal wedding."

My mother didn't think Muli was beautiful enough to match her smart and handsome son. She thought I could have done better. She saw many beautiful women attend my concerts and write notes of interest. She frequently asked, "Why would you pick someone so common?"

My conservative mother also wondered about Muli's moral values —she had already been engaged, spoken for by another. Was I receiving a woman who had been used and rejected?

Muli's jealous streak and controlling personality did not rest well with my mother. Muli—and my mother—had seen many beautiful women swoon at my music and chase me for autographs after my concerts. Muli worked vigilantly to keep them at arm's length.

My friends use to joke, "Ma, before Muli, you were energetic, proud, and self-confident. Now you act like a soldier lost in battle."

~

Muli also ran every facet of our day-to-day life, including reading and responding to my fan mail, which grew to hundreds of letters per week. When my mother asked my older brother, Siwu, to act as my part-time business manager, Muli reluctantly agreed. However, she insisted on having the final word on all musical and personal matters, including the first read of my fan mail.

My mother also had concerns about Muli being the featured pianist at my recitals. She felt Muli's piano skills were not up to the standards of my violin playing or my compositions. Occasionally, she would state her strong opinion in the form of a question: "Ma, are you satisfied with your piano accompaniment?"

I tried never to answer my mother's objections. I knew she was acting in what she thought was the best interest of her son. Changing her opinion on virtually anything to do with Muli could cause conflict; I always found conflict creatively counter-productive.

~

As for me, I was happy with the status quo; a conventional marriage was never an option. I grew up in Paris, not China. My artistic colleagues never discussed the concept of marriage, so I had no frame of reference. Either you were or you weren't in a relationship. Formal commitments were unstated; love was the basis of a relationship, not a reason to marry. And affairs during a relationship were not considered uncommon.

In fairness, Muli did ask about marriage on several l occasions; I ignored her requests, and that usually brought closure. Professionally, we collaborated seamlessly during our first years together. My concerts were generally flawless, and we were in high demand. I would estimate that we performed more than 40 recitals in Hong Kong, Shanghai, Being, Nanking, and other Asian cities. Muli was by my side every step of the way.

Like every relationship between a man and a woman, things were not always perfect. There were times when I would have preferred a more relaxed partnership. That desire for someone else led to a casual introduction to a lady you will meet later. We had a private consensual affair between the birth of my two daughters with Muli. Suffice to say, when Muli discovered my indiscretion, our relationship became strained, but it wasn't the end of our family, our musical collaboration, or our life partnership.

Chapter 16.

Trouble in Shanghai

上海的麻烦

Shanghai Hotel turns into a place Ma never forgets.

While I was not much interested in politics, I did believe that China deserved to be a united republic respected by the world. As my father said on many occasions, "The imperialists must go for the Chinese to find a new way forward." The question was how and when—that I left to my father and his fellow friends and revolutionaries.

~

During the 1930s, I felt my concerts took place in the violent shadow of an uneasy truce between the leaders of the nation's two competing parties, the Communists and Kuomintang (Nationalist Party), designed to bring Japan's aggressive behavior under control. In 1931, Japan invaded Manchuria, causing many Chinese residents to flee. Their goal was to avoid a united China. The Japanese feared a powerful China would make it more difficult to maintain political and military influence, and unlimited access to raw materials, food, and labor. During the next six years, the internal Chinese truce limited Japanese imperialist battles to small local skirmishes. But everyone knew it was just a matter of time before full-scale war broke out.

These events caused my music to take an unforeseen direction. I began to write war songs, incubated by distant bomb explosions, real and imagined. I composed my first war piece, *China's Soldiers*, in 1936 in Shanghai—it was a simple song of unity with four-part harmony. Two days later, the Central University Chorus performed the piece in public for the first time. I never imagined this quickly composed song could receive much fanfare, but when I played it at my future recitals, audiences asked for more.

I obliged by writing more war songs, including *A Bugle Call for Freedom* and *The Battle Song*.

Again, the audience reaction was surprising. I stopped to consider what was happening. I realized war songs were meant to be sung by the general public. But the Chinese people's musical level was quite low at the time, so my song structure and technique had to make it easy for the audience to sing without being childish or shallow, or sounding like a copy of a nationalistic German or American song. War songs have their own cultural identity. Every nation has a unique character; this is especially obvious in its music. Anti-Japan war songs are part of the soul of our nation. If it is not original, that says our country cannot be independent. Given my education in pure classical music, I realized Chinese music was built on weak foundations. To create strong, bold, nationalistic war songs, much needed to be discarded, and unexpected elements added. Fortunately, our folk songs are plentiful. This rich heritage nourished my compositions.

~

One day, in the middle of the growing uncertainty, a lively young man came to my house. He said he represented China Council, which wanted a few war songs from me. Songs that he could not only sing himself, but that he could teach others, and he wanted them right away to boost the morale of the soldiers and our citizens. But he wanted them immediately, so I opened my drawer, took out a few songs I had not performed in public, and handed to him.

From then on, the young man came to me often. I created custom-made songs to fill his needs, as well as "emergency songs" for unplanned moments. In time, there were so many requests that I committed more significant amounts of time than I ever imagined.

The young man told me my songs became best friends for soldiers fighting in the frontier as well as those working in support. They made our soldiers feel less desolate in the wild country, more courageous in battle, and more hopeful when they rested. I was overwhelmed with a sense of pride in my homeland.

~

In the summer of 1937, a dispute over control of the Marco Polo Bridge near the entrance to Beijing city center escalated into a full-scale battle that spread to many other parts of China. Living in Guangzhou was just like living on the frontline. Bombs shook the whole environment; living in the city was an adventure. No one could guarantee survival; a street you walked on one day to pick flowers was rubble the next day.

Most of my anti-Japanese war songs were created between January and February 1938. Each was designed to support the enormous fighting spirit of our people, who had endured so much. I wrote about 20 songs of war, including *Marching Forward!*, *Song of Guerrilla, Charge!*, and *Let's Take Up Arms to Defend South China*. I also wrote a memorial song, *This is not Death, but Eternal Life,* to praise those brave soldiers who sacrificed their lives to defend our nation.[2]

"Most of the lyrics for my war songs were picked from newly published poetry books of unknown, enthusiastic youths. Those lyrics are not deep, not grand, sometimes they read more like slogans. But the words are innocent, lively, and faithful. Occasionally the verses were too loose or long, and I had to act as repairmen to fix the song.

"On the accompaniments, I used vocal and melody to distinguish the lyrics' spirits. For example, in The Bugle Call for Freedom, the trumpet continuously blows throughout the song, in Marching Forward!' the sound of the soldiers' footsteps move from distance to close, in Charge! I used the augmented triad descending melody to express charging action".

~

By 1938, the Japanese had captured Beijing, Shanghai, and the Chinese capital of Nanking, forcing the Chinese central government to relocate to Chongqing (*chung-king*) in the Chinese interior. I had to resign my teaching job at Nanjing Central University and move to a professorship at Sun Yat-sen University in Guangzhou, a distance from the immediate military fighting.

By 1939, the fighting reached a stalemate. While Japan ruled the large cities, it lacked sufficient human resources to control China's vast countryside. During these years, I rarely saw my father. He always seemed to be in the middle of unstated pro-Chinese political activities at the New Asia Hotel, the unofficial headquarters for so-called strategic planning and mayhem.

---

[2] This passage is from the notes of Ma kept by his family more than 50 years. Here he explains how he combined the music and lyrics for his war songs. These notes are being made public for the first time in history.

Ironically, during these politically unstable times, I composed some of my best and work, including *Rondo No. 1 for Violin and Piano* and perhaps my most famous composition, *The Inner-Mongolian Suite.*[3]

~

In 1939, Muli gave birth to our first daughter, Ma Bixue, in Hong Kong. I was excited to tell my father, staying at the New Asia Hotel in Shanghai, where Muli and I had taught our private students. With luck, my father would get to meet his first granddaughter. When we arrived, I called his room, but there was no answer. I knocked on the door. When I entered, the police were searching the room. They said my father had been shot dead in the back of the head. They said there were no signs of a struggle, so the police assumed my father probably knew his assassin, which should narrow the search for the killer.

Father was only 56. I was crushed, angry, and bitter. Due to murky political circumstances at the time, the mystery of his death was never solved. But I have always believed that nobody *wanted* to solve the mystery of his death!

Over the years, three different theories have been offered about my father's assassination. Still, because China remains a limited human rights society, it is unlikely the case will ever be solved. Specifically:

1. My father had different ideas about the new Republic of China from other revolutionary leaders. As a scholar and thinker, he was convinced he was correct and never stopped promoting his ideas for a unified Republic of China. In the process, his dogged determination made him as many enemies as friends.

2. Chiang Kai-shek wanted him to negotiate a peace deal with the Japanese. He and my father probably agreed on the essential terms, but Chiang later changed his mind. My father protested, believing

---

[3] *Nostalgia,* the slow movement contained within the Mongolian Suite is the most beloved musical masterpiece in China, similar to the world's love for Claude Monet's mastepiece, *Water Lilies.*

Chiang's new terms would create corrupt financial benefits for a greedy few. Chiang did not want to debate the issue publicly, so he silenced my father by having him eliminated.

3. Chiang's rival, Wang Jingwei (*wan-cing-way*), wanted Ma Yuhang to work for him. My father refused, citing philosophical differences. Rather than face the public shame of rejection, Chiang had my father eliminated.

~

As the Americans say, the bottom line is that my father's assassination brought a depressing reality. Despite all his grand words, Chiang Kai-Shek was no different from many of China's past power-hungry warlords. Chiang's original mission—to have all Chinese share in the country's enormous resources and make China a proud and independent country—was swallowed up by the visible corruption and greed within every level of the Chinese Nationalist Party (KMT).

Chapter 17.

Traveling Shu Road

行蜀路

Artists rending of the steep 2,000 Chinese passageway
(Courtesy Metropolitan Museum of Art)

As a father with a family, it was my responsibility to locate a place that offered some measure of peace and stability. Muli and I decided to move to Hong Kong, which was part of the British Empire and not under direct attack or occupation by the Japanese.

However, we quickly learned life in Hong Kong was more difficult than we initially imagined. The proximity of Hong Kong to Mainland China and the continued threats of collateral damage from the nearby Japanese aggression had their consequences on everyday life in Hong Kong.

Shortages, real and imagined, created runaway inflation; food prices seemed to increase a couple of times a day. I also struggled to earn enough money to make ends meet and deal with a chronically unhappy wife who wished the war would just go away. My only outlet for inner peace and tranquility was composing music.

Ironically, despite our desperate circumstances, I completed one of my more emotionally confident compositions, *F Major String Quartet No. 1*. I remember wondering when I finished the piece, what force within caused this burst of artistic energy? At 27, I was still learning about myself.

~

Soon, I received some good news. I was offered a musical professorship at Sun Yat-sen University in Yunnan province (southwestern China), near the capital city of Kunming (kun-ying).

Muli asked, "How much will you be paid?"

I answered her question with a story. "As the professor walked down the street, a thief started to follow him. The professor noticed the man, and he turned and said, 'I am a professor.' The thief knew that he found the wrong target and walked away."

Muli glared. "Are you telling me your salary will just provide the basics?"

I chose to show Muli a topographical map. "The area appears to be filled with many beautiful hills and valleys."

She realized the professorship was essential to me, so she became optimistically practical, "Well, at least the prices will be lower than the hell of Hong Kong!"

I let things be. I did not disclose that the University was over 730 miles away.

~

Soon Muli, our new first daughter Ma Bixue (*ma-be-sway*), and I began the four-day journey from Hong Kong to Kunming, traveling aboard an old, crowded wooden ship that sailed through the choppy South Seas and docked in Haiphong, Vietnam. We traveled light with just a few essentials.

From Haiphong, we took two trains over poor railbeds, then three buses on dusty, bumpy dirt roads. Finally, we reached the campus in Chengjiang (*cheng-sauce*), which turned out to be a small town in a mountain valley, 40 miles from Kunming city center.

As expected, the small campus was surrounded by beautiful rolling hills filled with colorful wild roses, apple blossoms, and brightly colored butterflies. But the classrooms and living facilities were nothing more than a collection of tiny, shabby buildings with no electricity or running water. Baby Bixue quickly developed a routine. She began crying about midnight, and I would get up to retrieve her. Then, under a dimly lit oil lamp, I would pace back and forth, softly rocking her and singing until she fell back to sleep.

I had to laugh at my situation. In a matter of a few years, I had gone from a respected violin virtuoso in Paris to a 27-year-old father living in a town even the Chinese had a hard time finding on a map. During my private moments surrounded by nature, I composed what critics would eventually call, "one my most lyrical compositions," *Rondo No. 1 for Violin and Piano.*

We quickly discovered there was no place in Chengjiang *(cheng sauce)* to give violin performances. So Muli and I agreed to move to again. She wanted safety for us and opportunity for me. She understood my gifts and was a willing partner. After some deliberation, we decided to live in Chongqing (*chong-chi*), the provisional capital of the Republic of China, a bustling city in southwest China that sat at the confluence of two major rivers—the Yangtze and Jialing. Chongqing was a major river port, transportation hub, and commercial and industrial center. Most importantly, the city had radio stations, recital halls, and several performing orchestras.

~

Traveling to Chongqing in February was far more challenging than either of us initially imagined. The central part of the trip required traveling the Shu Route, a 2,000-year-old passageway that twisted around mountains on unmarked dirt roads so narrow they were breathtaking. Amazing Muli slept peacefully while I held Bixue firmly in my grasp and stared out the window. At that moment, I understood the truth of the famous Chinese poem, *The Difficulty of the Shu Road.*

> Ooh ah etc.
> So dangerous, so high!
> The difficulty of the Shu Road,
> As difficult as climbing to the blue sky!...
> ...Up to today, it has been forty-eight thousand years,
> Yet on this path to Qin, there has not been a sign of people.
> To the west, on Mt Taibai, is a way only for birds, that crosses to the summit of Mt. E'Mei.
> And only then was this road in the sky linked with a plank road.
> The ground collapsed, and the mountain crumbled-warrior heroes die.
>
> ~

After several days, the bus reached Chongqing. The city was alive and bustling; I was quickly recognized as the "violin virtuoso with the black eyeballs." Muli and I gave a violin and piano recital, which was broadcast on the radio. The reviews were outstanding; soon, I had two conductor jobs and a hectic recital schedule. The national government also asked me to give more recitals so that ticket sales could be used to purchase military equipment and supplies to fight the Japanese. While I never found out how much money was raised, all six recitals were sold out.

In 1940, the Central Movie Studio made a film called *Tibet Parade*, which introduced a humorous Tibetan ritual in which the Dalai and Panchen Lamas have to sit on the bed of their predecessor before they can be enthroned. I was asked to compose ten pieces of music for the film, three of which I later reused in my *Inner Mongolia Suite*, *Tone Poem of Tibet*, and *Madrigal*, all for violin and piano.

During our stay in Chongqing, the population exploded; high ranking Kuomintang (*ko-min-ten*) officials were everywhere, and the prices for everything skyrocketed. And for the first time, the Communist Party leader Zhou Enlai had his underground communities contact me for help financially against the Japanese, and to elude Kuomintang. Before long, I was helping them communicate by hiding messages in my violin case while on tour. Working for the government also allowed me to see crony capitalism up close. I was disgusted that the people once again came last. I decided it was time for Muli and me to move to Hong Kong again which, while under British control, remained stable and free from Japanese air raids.

Chapter 18.

Home Sweet Home

家, 甜蜜的家

Ma's family home in Haifeng, Guangdong Province

In summer 1941, Muli, Bixue, and I arrived in Hong Kong. We soon gave recitals at the Grand Empress Theater in the Peninsula Hotel, among other landmark venues. The ticket sales and prices were excellent, which let us afford a comfortable life. I also made extra income teaching private students at home.

I also tried not to forget about our armed forces fighting the Japanese under challenging conditions. From time to time, I would send money to Chiang Kai-shek's chief of staff. It was the least I could do to contribute to my homeland, the Republic of China. The stable times also allowed me to complete a major new work, *E Major Symphony No. 1.*, a bold, energetic, joyful piece designed to make the listener's emotions soar. When the work was complete, I realized I had learned much about the process of symphony development and was confident I could incorporate those insights into the appropriate future compositions.[4]

"First, you need to have intent. This intent is not necessarily as clear as literature, but it can be straightforward. For example, I want to express "spring" but without complex content or story. It is just a perception in my mind; then, I will use a suitable music style to show it.

"Of course, the subject matter can have many ways to treat it, but first, it has to strike a chord in people's hearts, and the melody is pleasant on the ear.

"A symphony proceeds with two processes. A static process where the music stays in a similar style melody for a more extended period. The evolving process where the music's melody style changes. The change needs to follow specific rules; otherwise, the music becomes disarray."

~

Our peaceful life in Hong Kong ended suddenly on December 9, 1941. An unimaginable headline appeared in the Hong Kong papers: "Japan Sneak Attacks American Pearl Harbor Naval Base."

As I read the story, I began to hear sirens. Japanese warplanes filled the sky; it was raining bombs, and the Brits did not have the firepower to stop them. Paradise had turned into hell. Soon, Japan bombed Wake Island, Guam, Singapore, Manila. All of Southeast Asia was in ruin.

For the next eight days and nights, we were hungry refugees seeking shelter, along with so many others. Muli and I wondered where we could go. We decided my hometown of Haifeng was an unlikely target of the Japanese aggressors. I assumed Japan's military

---

[4] Notes from Ma diaries about his process of symphonic development.

forces only had the bandwidth to terrorize China's larger cities, thus sparing vast amounts of the countryside and small towns. We fled Hong Kong in darkness with a few clothes and whatever money we had saved.

~

We arrived in Haifeng at the start of the spring festival time. The bustling Lungjin (*long-jin*) River was still and quiet—but there were no dragon boats, colorful vendors, or lively crowds on the riverbanks. As we walked down Shi street to my family home, every door was tightly shut, and the usual red spring couplets (decorations) were missing.

As we entered the gate, the first people to welcome us were my auntie and four cousins. Auntie said, "The war has destroyed the family business. Siwu has left to teach outside our hometown, but Siqui now runs a modest trading business with the help of your mother and sisters."

~

I took Muli on a personal guided tour of Haifeng: one movie theater, two food stores, and an old photography shop. I remember joking, "As you can see, Haifeng is not an international hub like Shanghai. We don't have any French, German, or British residents."

"Where is the beach?" Muli asked. She remembered the story about the white sand beach where I had learned to swim. "As I recall," she said, "your mother told me you were famous for missing school because it was boring."

I said, "You have a good memory. Mother came out of the bushes, right over there, and took me back to school." Muli smiled in a way I hadn't seen in some time; I realized how much we had already shared and the many unplanned experiences we had yet to share.

~

While we were in Haifeng, Muli and I performed several fundraising recitals for the war efforts. People formed long lines to purchase tickets. As one old friend said, "I can't wait to hear our hometown hero. The papers report you are becoming quite famous."

I just nodded; I was uncomfortable talking about myself in such terms.

~

After one fundraising violin and piano recital, I asked Muli, "Are you hungry?"

"Yes, of course," replied Muli.

"Then, I will treat you to p-ko, Haifeng's most delicious and famous dessert." I took her hand and walked toward the lighted night market.

"Haifeng has a famous dessert!" said Muli.

"Wait and see," I smiled. "The dessert is so delicious; one bowl will not be enough." Once inside the store, I called out to the old man behind the counter, "Two small bowls of sesame paste soup." The elderly man brought over two large bowls. I explained, "Oh, no, not large bowls, we want small bowls."

"How can you have enough if you eat only small bowls?" replied the old man.

"It's okay," said Muli. "Large bowls are fine."

The man placed two unappetizing bowls of grayish soup on the table. Muli refused to try it.

"Just one spoon," I begged. "Promise."

She put one spoon in her mouth and was pleasantly surprised. "OOOH! It tastes delicious!" I began to eat my bowl, but the sesame paste seemed sweeter than I remembered.

I smiled courteously. "Have you added more sugar than usual?" The man replied, "Special recipe."

Then he brought two more large bowls of the sesame paste and placed them in front of us. Muli smiled raised her hand, "Lao yeye! [respectful Chinese nickname for an old man] My husband and I have had enough!"

The old man pointed to a wok on the stove. "There, I have a full wok of sesame paste soup. Eat more! Eat more! It is all on me, even if you finish the whole wok."

"Why would you do that? Aren't you in business to make a profit?" I replied.

The old man smiled with a twinkle in his eye. "Yesterday I went to a violin concert at the university. So as soon as you walked into my store, I realized you were the famous violinist. I am proud you are my customer."

"Do you know my violin music?" I asked.

"One of the pieces sounded like parade music, but it was difficult for me to understand fully. However, your song *Longing for Home*—I loved that one."

"Haoting! Haoting! [Pleased to hear] You make my wife and I feel proud." Muli nodded in agreement.

When we finished eating, Muli tried to place some money in the old man's hand, but he waved her off. "Like said, on me."

I remembered I had two tickets for tomorrow's concert in my pocket. I handed them to the old man, who happily accepted.

As we left that store, a cold breeze slapped my face. It was a reminder that my countrymen were suffering at the hands of the Japanese, and it was my duty to support them with more recitals. For 5,000 years, the Chinese have relied on each other to survive the troubling moments in our proud history. I was confident the Japanese would soon learn that lesson.

~

While in Haifeng, I became intrigued with local opera music. To learn more, my cousin invited a well-respected local artist to our home. The man played several local works on his two-stringed erhu-hu (Chinese violin). I was fascinated by what I saw and began taking pages of notes.

The surprised artist said, "What are you doing?"

I asked the man for his erhu and repeated the pieces.

"Mr. Ma," he said, " In Haifeng, when I teach my students, each piece takes three years to master. You are too fast! If I took you as my student, you would learn all my tricks, and I would be out of a job. Nobody will ask me to teach them. Of course, if I were lucky enough to have a student like you—a French-educated musician and a university professor—it would be the most glorious moment in my life."

The artist continued to play, and I continued to take notes.

~

I received a letter from an artist friend who lived in Guilin to the south two months later. Guilin, known for its majestic limestone hills, was appreciated for its support of arts and culture. "Ma, I am certain that a man of your gifts will find many musical opportunities. And there are no Japanese in sight!"

It was time to leave my sweet, seafront Haifeng for a second time. Without hesitation, Muli packed our belongings, and we said our goodbyes. Family tears were everywhere. We had no idea if or when we might see each other again.

Chapter 19.

90 Days in Guilin

桂林90天

Ma (lower left) and Muli (center) formed a classical quartet in Guilin(quay-lynn)

When we arrived in Guilin, I was physically and emotionally exhausted from the strain of war, refugees in flight, and my urgency to expand musical boundaries and my obligations as a father and breadwinner.

Fortunately, Guilin turned out to be the perfect place to unwind; I gained inspiration from the beauty of nature and from concentrating on performing, not composing. We also decided to donate a portion of ticket sales to create a charitable organization to help other war refugees.

Muli went from being a mother and my accompanist to our booking agent, public affairs manager, and fan club manager. We performed in numerous venues, nearby universities, and music halls, receiving positive reviews and publicity that found its way around China's cities.

One of my dear friends, the poet Xu Chi, learned of my presence in Guilin. He proposed I write a series of letters about my artistic philosophies.

I laughed. "Who would want to read such a thing?"

His response surprised me. "Everybody wants to hear the words of a national treasure." The praise seemed lofty at the time. But it was the way the people and the government did come to think of me!

Muli agreed with Xu Chi. But she had a different motivation for the letters. "They will be good publicity to help us book recitals and sell tickets." Subsequently, the letters were published in the highly respected *Ta Kong*, my country's oldest Chinese-language newspaper, founded in 1902.

In the first letter, titled *Purely Music*, I wrote:

> "Music directly calls out some particular emotion, but it does not explain why a specific passion is called out. Music only calls out a result; it does not care about the origin. Individuals depend on their own experiences and memories to make associations. Therefore, everyone has one's interpretations, but it is not possible those interpretations are the same.
>
> "Because music can call out associations, some composers determine the particular associations, produce music titles. I disagree; if you remove the title, what's left is pure music, which again calls out different associations

depending on the individual. To me, pure music is better than titled music because it can forever call out new associations."

To my surprise, despite the ongoing war, I received numerous pieces of fan mail. Muli made sure she opened each piece and responded to remind the writer of my next appearance. I wasn't interested in ticket sales; I was a musician, not a businessman. But I must admit that Muli was right. Ticket sales increased, and we donated more to the cause. I also heard from a few of my artist friends who said they read the piece with interest and wondered if there would be more.

So I wrote another. The letter was entitled *Dance, Opera, Internationality, and Nationality*:

"Music adds motion and words to form opera, which, for me, is music is at the highest level for expression. However, dance and opera are also considered by people as perfect art forms. In music history, an opera is an art form that has done the most to attract people to the musical circle. I hope, in the future, I will be able to compose such works.

"Concerning music's relationship to internationality, nationality, and individual relationships, I believe music can have individuality without the necessity for nationality and international influence. But at the highest level, music probably contains all three."

The results were much the same. Everyone was pleased. As for me, I realized, perhaps for the first time, that I needed to maintain my humble, dignified origins as my moral compass, regardless of my successes.

~

In the summer of 1942, a group of my family and friends—all well-known artists in their fields—spent two days and one night on a sailboat on the azure lakes near the limestone slopes. It was a pleasant break from the war. During the day, we swam, fished, and told our individual war stories filled with risk and danger. Swimming brought back memories of my childhood on the white sandy beaches near my childhood home.

That night, we sat around the campfire laughing, dancing, playing music, and barbecuing the fish. As the evening progressed, my friends lit torches under a crystal night sky filled with twinkling stars and asked me to play my violin. I had given many recitals to many audiences, but this was a moment of inner tranquility I would never forget. It was as though time stood still. I thought of my gift and how happy it made people. I could ask no more out of life. I was a fortunate man. The next day, Muli and I agreed that family and friends were everything; we talked of adding another child to our family. Life was good, despite the war.

Later that same summer, Muli and I gave a recital which was broadcast live on the radio from the Guilin stage where we were performing. Suddenly, there was a power outage; the lights shut down, and the stage was in total darkness. Muli and I were forced to stop playing, unsure of what to do. The audience sat patiently waiting, assuming the lights would return. Some time went by, and everyone remained in darkness. Muli and I got up and were about to leave the stage when a single flashlight shined toward us. Soon, ten more flashlights followed. Muli nodded; we continued the recital. The longer we played, the more flashlights seemed to light up. The audience was so polite and respectful; we decided to play multiple encores as a thank you.

~

Muli, Bixue, and I returned to the Sun Yat-sen University in early autumn, located in Pingshi (*ping-she*), Guangdong. There, I would teach music, compose, hold recitals, and expand our family. By spring, Muli was pregnant, with an expected delivery date of August.

Chapter 20.

Unfaithful

不忠

Sun Yat-sen University, where Ma made a big mistake.

Sometimes a man makes a mistake and never recovers. I was more fortunate than most. However, it is now many years later, and time to apologize to Muli publicly. I hope my grandchildren understand.

~

Before my now pregnant Muli and I returned to Sun Yat-sen University in late 1942, we left our daughter, Bixue, with my third auntie. We asked Auntie to take Bixue to live with Grandma in

Shanghai, the only major Chinese city left untouched by the fighting because of the presence of tens of thousands of French, German, and British nationals.

Without a child to worry about, we were able to increase our recital schedule and, as always, donate part of the proceeds to the war effort. Despite the difficult times, I could see the patriotic pride on the faces of my audiences. They knew one of their own had become a renowned violin virtuoso.

The positive energy I felt teaching at Pingshi *(pin-she)* also encouraged me to take some composition risks I might not otherwise have considered.

I recalled my work with the Chinese Central Movie Studio, for whom I had composed a ten-piece music score for a film called *Tibet Parade,* which introduced the country's fifteenth Dalai Lama. I decided to write my darkest, most depressing work, the *Tibetan Tone Violin Suite,* using three of those pieces as movements.

The first movement contained dark, terrifying chords, which created images of a wild beast on the run. The second movement was a sad funeral procession that used the melody in the popular Tibetan folk song. The third movement praised the violent power of the sword and the beauty of love.

After some months, the piece was ready for recital debut. By then, Muli's pregnancy left her constantly tired. We rarely had relations. Despite having needs, I did not force the issue. Muli was not a large woman, and the constant travel and busy schedule had worn on her. For one of the few times in our careers, Muli could not perform; she was dizzy, and her stomach ached. "I would suggest you find a replacement to accompany you. I believe that would be best," she said. I agreed.

~

The word went out at the university that I was looking for a piano accompanist. I listened to many musicians, but none met my standards. I was about to make adjustments to perform solo when an attractive, well-dressed woman entered. Like Muli, she seemed more European than Chinese. And, like Muli, she was quietly self-confident. In her case, that was with reason—she was outstanding. After playing one of her compositions, we rehearsed one of my pieces. It was as though we had played together for a long time. I could feel the professional chemistry.

The sold-out performance went very well that evening. I was pleased with the concert and the audience's reaction.

When everybody had left, she approached. "*You* are wonderful." "I'm glad you enjoyed performing," I replied.

She smiled. "That was good, also."

Soon, we were sipping tea at a small café when she asked an odd question. "I'm a member of the Communist Party; what about you?"

"I'm not a member of any party," I replied. "I want nothing to do with politics. I am a musician."

"I don't understand; how do you receive such government support?" she asked.

"The government knows I play for the pride of the Chinese people. And for the United Republic of China."

"I have never met a person with such high ideals," she said wistfully. I placed my hand on the table to pour more tea; she put her hand in mine. I felt physical urges but tried to dismiss them.

"It's getting late," she said, "Would you like to visit my home?" I hesitated.

"She'll never know," she whispered. I knew the proper answer was no. But I was weak and gave in to temptation. We spent several hours making love before I returned home in the middle of the night. Fortunately, when I arrived, Muli was sleeping.

For the next few months, we shared many discreet liaisons as time and place permitted. Since Muli said nothing, I assumed my unfaithful behavior was safely undiscovered.

One day, Muli and I were sitting in our courtyard having tea. The sun streamed through the trees. As Muli poured, she asked, "How does *she* like her tea?"

Chapter 21.

Regaining Muli's Trust

重新获得慕理的信任

Ma and his second daughter Ruixue (ce-llee-a).

The affair cost me dearly—I lost Muli's trust. I know she wondered if this woman was the only one. But protestations of innocence would only make things worse with a justifiably suspicious wife like Muli. I decided to make amends to be the best husband and father I could be and say nothing more about the affair unless asked. I could feel Muli's ever-vigilant eyes watch my behavior on and off the stage. She also made it her business not to let any woman come in close contact with me.

~

In August 1943, three months after my indiscretion ended, our second daughter, Celia, was born in the small town of Bingshi, not far from the University. Due to hardships of war and lack of proper nutrition, she was undersized—five and a half pounds at birth—and her whole body was covered with infant's hairs. I would tell Muli, "Holding Celia was like holding a tiny mouse." Muli did not find the observation funny.

Celia cried constantly. But we discovered that when I stirred sugar water in a glass to improve her nutrition, Celia would hear a spoon hitting the glass side and stop crying. We both found her little trick amusing.

~

Bingshi was an exceptionally tranquil place near a beautiful forest, with a winding river stocked with songbirds and small, cute animals. We lived in a simple house on the mountain top covered with colorful azaleas in the spring.

Our temporary quarters were relatively modest, but Muli made it feel like a home. She even created a study room for me. The birds never seemed to stop singing whenever I was busy writing music, so we named my study *Ting Niao Zhang* (the Bird Chirping Room).

In spring, Muli and I performed violin and piano recitals at our house. The students decorated the stage with azaleas and the visitors, traveling at night, held torches to light their way. The winding torches looked like a huge fire dragon gliding through the mountain roads as I stood in front of our house.

In this tranquil environment, I composed Violin Concerto in F Major, which expressed the need to have faith and hope because good times will come.

I created the piece with three distinct movements that contained popular Guangdong local folk musical elements blended with Western traditions to form my style. My goal was to create an emotionally uplifting three-movement concerto that spoke of my birthplace, the carefree days of youth, and my optimism for a happy, prosperous China. Based on the audience reception and press coverage, I was pleased to have achieved my objective. At that moment, I had no idea my imaginative integration of these Chinese and Western melodies would carry me to heights few classical artists ever achieve, then cause me to flee my country as an enemy of the state.

~

By 1944, the Sino-Japanese war entered a challenging phase. The now desperate Japanese intensified their assaults against our people with relentless, violent air raids. Muli and I spent seven months visiting Chinese military camps, giving free concerts to lift our soldiers' spirits and encourage them to continue to resist Japan's aggression. The audiences especially loved music with Chinese favors; sometimes, they forgot they were outside standing in the bitter cold during our performances.

As Americans well know, the actor-comedian Bob Hope gained much notoriety for taking traveling shows to American soldiers. I was the Chinese version in some ways, but our recitals did not contain big band music, funny jokes, or scantily clad women. That is not the Chinese way!

~

During our stay at Sun Yat-sen University, Muli, Celia, and I moved four times as areas fell under Japanese control, creating countless refugees, including ourselves. The scenes of suffering we saw firsthand were horrible as we struggled through muddy and slushy roads. When there was a break in the action, I took it upon myself to perform free for those exhausted refugees.

I always worried about Muli's and Celia's safety. Often, we were unable to reach towns that had rooms for rent, so we spent many nights in roadside homes of peasant villagers. I found great joy in the attitude of these loving, honest, simple people.

When we reached the larger cities, we again gave concerts that offered comfort and hope and donated significant ticket revenues to charities for other refugees.

Eventually, Muli and I reached Kunming, the capital city of Yunnan, a place well known for its natural beauty. Chinese people often refer to it as "paradise on earth." Its subtropical geographic location and high latitude make its weather mild, and its mountain ranges were covered with varieties of colorful flowers, many unknown in the Western world.

As I stood lakeside, with rhododendron-laced hills in the background, I was mesmerized by the white junk boats puttering across the mirror glass waters and the yellow willow trees swaying on the shore. All of my journey's exhaustion seemed to wash away; I felt refreshed.

This feast for the eyes inspired me to compose two merry and festive pieces, *Pastorale for Violin* and *Autumn Harvest Dance*, which expressed my new, changed mood and mindset about music composition.

While in Kunming, I published another letter on my changing view of music. In part, it read:

"Chinese music, like Chinese culture, is at the cross-points of two rivers. It is no longer the earlier river; it is a new river. While it contains the old rivers' waters, it is an entirely new river and different from the two older rivers.

Chinese culture embedded in its music may appear to lose its original character because of outside influence. But that is not the case; we will not lose our national spirit.

On the contrary, we will obtain an even more valuable national spirit because it will be fresher, more specific music. The key to creating depends on our musician's endeavor to learn Western techniques and learn from the land, mountain, plain, river of our civilians.

New Chinese music is not going to be for the few; it will be embedded in millions of Chinese hearts."

~

I was right. My new vision of Chinese music became the focus of another series of concerts for the war effort. Almost every civilian bought tickets, as well as local dignitaries and the state governor. Ticket sales reached huge numbers. A friend observed the sales and cracked a joke, which offended me deeply. "Ma, you have made so much money on ticket sales you can afford whatever you want for your whole life!"

I replied curtly, "What I do, I do for our people and our country. The money goes to China's Women & Children Rescue Fund, not to me."

The man realized he had made a terrible mistake. "Ma, I am so sorry. How can I fix my mistake?"

I smiled. "Buy more tickets."

~

In February 1945, my family and I journeyed to the national capital, Chungking, where we again gave any concerts for the cause. One of the highlights for me was my partnership with the respected Zhonghua *(jong-faa)* Symphony Orchestra to perform my *Symphony No. 1.*

After Chengdu, I could feel my health deteriorating. I needed rest, so my family and I went into seclusion at a small village that possessed nature beauty with an attractive landscape, abundant refresh foods, and kind, innocent villagers.

On September 9, 1945, the news that the Sino-Japanese war was over left the whole of China in a celebratory mood, captured in a poem by the well-known Du Fu (*doe-foo*).

> Just heard the news,
> Happy tears wetted my clothes.
> My wife and children,
> Where are your worries?
> Put together poetry and books, I sing, I drink
> all day long. My youth is my companion,
> Good time for me to return to the homeland.

~

During these trying formative years, Celia's personality began to develop; she had her mother's determination. When Celia was two years old, she wanted a cat for a pet. Muli was not thrilled about the idea since the house was small. But Celia insisted, so I took her to look in the village shops for a cat to buy. Celia was incredibly fussy; she made me walk from one pet store to another until she found "the perfect" yellow-striped cat that looked like a small tiger.

Celia named it Master. Master proved to be a perfect cat. He was so active and diligent that all the mice in the neighborhood disappeared shortly after his arrival.

One day, Master stopped eating and looked like he was dying. Celia cried. "Daddy, why is he so sick?"

I replied, "Master may have eaten too many mice." I told her not to worry; I had a secret medicine. I broke an orange skin into small pieces and force-fed them to Master. In no time, Master spit out lots of mouse hair and bones on the way to his full recovery.

The Master incident was the only time Muli referred to my previous affair. After the cat recovered, she looked at me and said, "If only all unpleasant things could be removed that easily."

~

On September 9, 1945, the Japanese officially surrendered to

China. The Sino-Japanese war was over after seven years of bitter fighting and bloodshed. Generalissimo Chiang Kai-shek and his Kuomintang party, who led the successful fight against the Japanese, decided to have a victory celebration event at Chongqing's war capital.

Chiang, well aware of my contributions to the Republic, invited me to perform. I readily accepted the honor, not realizing the Kuomintang high officials knew nothing about solo violin recitals. They thought the violin recitals were like the Chinese opera, where it was acceptable for patrons to chat, drink tea, and sip on watermelon seeds during the performance.

As I walked on stage, I witnessed inconsiderate behavior and noisy conversations. I retreated backstage and refused to perform. Chiang's Minister of Education, Zhen Lifu (cing-me-fen), rushed to my side and pleaded, "Generalissimo Chiang is waiting; please get on the stage and play."

"Not under these conditions," I said stubbornly. Zhen informed Chiang about the stalemate. Chiang immediately ordered his people to stop chatting, drinking and eating. After the place quieted down, I got on stage and played with passion.

~

A few months later, I received a letter from Siqui in Shanghai. "The war is over; it's time to celebrate, to get to know our families as they are today. I suggest we hold a family reunion at a place we all know, the New Asia Hotel in Shanghai."

Muli and I agreed. Of all the places we had lived, Shanghai was her favorite. I resigned from my art curator position in Chungking and boarded a ship that sailed on the Yangtze River and passed the Three Gorges landmark on the way to Shanghai. My thought was that we could start life anew in a city we loved.

Chapter 22.

Family Reunion

家庭团聚

Top: Ma (right) and brothers one, two, and three.
Bottom: Mother (center) and daughters.

The family reunion at the New Asia Hotel was a joyful gathering filled with cries and laughter in Haifeng, Mandarin, Cantonese, and Shanghai dialects, mixed with a few English and French phrases.

Ten years before, my younger brother, Si-Hon, had held his premiere violin recital at the hotel, which critics said had "established him as an emerging prodigy from the talented Ma family." Now 21, Si-Hon was well-respected throughout China. My younger sisters had also established themselves in the Chinese music world—sixth sister Sisun was a pianist, eighth sister Siju was a cellist, and tenth sister Siyun was a flutist. I told them, "As your older brother, I could not be prouder of your accomplishments."

My mother, aging but in good health, was now the family matriarch. She was happy to see that her children, wives, and grandchildren were safe and unscathed by the terrible war.

My older brothers, Siqui and Siwu, had built excellent careers in education in Shanghai, thanks to my father's foresight to have them study in France.

Siqui was now a professor at the Communication University of China, the country's leading school studying journalism and international communications. He and his wife, Li Wei (*low-way*), had a daughter and three sons, and he was a frequent contributor to the leading academic journals of the time.

Siwu, who developed his ear for language while studying in France, taught French and English, among other things, at the Foreign Language College in Shanghai. He was also the only family member with a European wife. Siqui decided to tease Siwu, "So Brother, tell us where you found such a beautiful Chinese woman?" Mother smiled at her elegant and fashionable daughter-in-law with porcelain white skin, long blonde hair, and bright blue eyes.

"It was love at first sight with Ma Zhuge," responded Siwu, proudly.

"For you or her?" laughed Siqui.

My blond-haired sister-in-law came to Siwu's rescue. "The first time I met your brother at my mother's house, I knew. He was handsome, energetic, and had a curious mind." Her tenacity reminded me of Muli.

Li Wei asked, "Sister, how did a blond European receive the name of a Chinese man?"

Siwu explained. "Before we married, I consulted with my trusted friends, Siqui and Sicong. They reminded me of the legend of Zhuge

Laing, the Chinese wise man who lived during the Three Kingdoms Period. He excelled as a politician, military strategist, writer, engineer, inventor, and astronomer. I decided her name should be Ma Zhuge because she was all of that and more." Ma Zhuge and Mother beamed.

~

Siqui, Siwu, and I spent time reminiscing about our happy times in France. My brothers recalled a little cafe we often visited in Bois Colombes, about five miles from Paris city center. The owner's daughter was the waitress. She was beautiful but very distant and without good manners. Every time she delivered a dish, she put it in front of them without a smile, said "voila" (there it is), and walked away.

Mother asked, "With such terrible service, why did you return?" They laughed. "The food was delicious and quite reasonable. We also gave her the nickname, "Mademoiselle Voilà," which she thought was rude. Ma Zhuge looked skeptically at her husband.

"The story is true," I said. "One day, my brothers took me to the bistro, and she came to the entrance to seat us," I said, "Bonjour Mademoiselle Voilà." She was mad as hell and walked away.

~

Siqui decided to share a story of mischief that involved me during the time I recuperated in Breck. "One day, while lounging on the beach, my little brother met twin brothers from the royal family of Hungary. They persuaded my naive Ma to join them in a little practical joke at the luxury home of a nearby neighbor. The three of them began throwing pebbles into the man's meticulous gardens. The owner came storming out. The twin brothers saw the man out of the corner of their eyes and fled. Ma was still tossing pebbles when the man came up behind him and grabbed him by the collar. Ma had to apologize to the owner and was made to write, 'I will never do that again' one hundred times with a white brushstroke. "

~

At that moment, my mind turned to thoughts of my father. I wondered why anyone would have assassinated such a wise, intelligent man. We had a moment of silence in tribute. Mother shed tears, something I rarely saw her do.

"And what about our gifted brother?" asked Siqui moments later. I did not wish to say much. My brothers insisted. "The war has forced Muli, Celia, and me to relocate many times—sometimes to places that seemed like hell. We have traveled on rough seas and difficult roads while trying to keep safe and create music. Sometimes, I look at a composition finished during these awkward moments and wonder, what unknown fountain did I tap within me?

"Sometimes we had food, other times, very little. I am sad to say little Celia has gone hungry more times than she deserved. But there have also been good moments. We have given recitals to appreciative audiences all over China, donated most of the proceeds to our battered forces, and given hope to the many refugees fleeing with little more than the clothes on their backs. The horrors we have seen, I would not wish upon a dog." The room was hushed. "I apologize for speaking too much."

Siqui responded, "No need, little brother. Your family is in awe of your accomplishments and your commitment to our homeland."

"Who knows," said Siqui, wryly. "Maybe someday there will be a postage stamp in your name or a museum filled with your works in Guangzhou."

I thought Siqui's comment absurd, so I responded with equal bravado. "And someday I will be crowned *The King of Violins!*"

My mother smiled, nodded, and walked over to me; she held me tight and whispered in my ear, "Father would have been proud." It had been a long time since she had held me in her warm, loving arms. I didn't realize how much I missed that feeling.

Chapter 23.

Zhou & Mao & Ma

周和毛和馬

Chairman Mao and Ma Sicong's buddy, Premier Zhou Enlai.

Shortly after the family reunion, Muli, Celia, and I returned to my hometown of Guangzhou. Soon, a terrible civil war broke out between Chiang Kai-shek's Nationalist Kuomintang Party (KMT) and the Communist Party led by the legendary Mao Zedong. The fighting reached the border of Guangzhou. I was tired of the endless wars and fled to the safety of Hong Kong with my family.

Three years later, the Communist armies prevailed, Chiang Kai-shek was forced to retreat to Taiwan, the People's Republic of China (PRC) was formed, and Mao Zedong was installed as Party Chairmen.

Once Chiang was gone, all of China seemed to accept the communist ascension. Public sentiment in the cities during that first year was one of euphoria. Residents saw the conquering army as a group of seemingly self-disciplined country lads who appeared helpful and polite—a stark contrast to the looting and raping activities by the warlords and often corrupt KMT troops.

The new government was seen as cleaning things up—the streets, the drains, the filth, garbage, petty criminals, prostitutes, and beggars.

All involved in criminal and immoral activities—however small—were rounded up and sent for reeducation to make them productive members of the new society.

Events in China moved faster than even Mao anticipated. The Communist Party had about 750,000 members, but there was a need to fill over two million government posts. Consequently, many KMT officials remained in their positions, drawing salaries and continuing their functions. At the same time, the new government abolished foreign privileges, stamped out corruption, and mobilized the citizenry into functional teams who repaired public works, spread literacy, serviced railroads, and repaired steamship lines.

Mao also realized China's rampant inflation of 100 percent and more had to end. The government took over the banking system to control credit activities and the creation of money. People were paid in essential commodities instead of cash. These drastic measures worked, and the rate of inflation dropped to 15 percent a year by 1953.

~

During this period of social upheaval, Muli and I settled in the peaceful city of Tianjin, 70 miles from Beijing, to establish the Central Conservatory of Music. I decided it was close enough to the city to recruit students yet far enough away from the day's politics.

Unlike so many of our past trips, the trip to Tianjin was relatively uneventful. We began with a silky-smooth sail to the coastal city of Yanai. That evening, we gathered on deck to enjoy the colorful summer sunset and the endless blue ocean. Later, we held a party in the hall cabin, which lasted long into the night. At Yanai, we climbed into bumpy train carriages with old broken locomotives. The train passed many lines of soldiers and made countless unscheduled stops, sometimes for hours, but no one cared.

I composed notable pieces such as Tribute of October and the grand chorus Yalu River during the next few years. But I spent most of my time building the school's capabilities and reputation, which left little time for composing. The search for qualified professors who met my standards was my priority. The construction of a student curriculum and various administrative matters from classroom size to the location and acoustics of recital space was a close second. Since much of what I was doing was new to me, it was like a massive dose of on-the-job training.

~

Shortly after the Conservatory opened to much local fanfare, Mao's Communist Party established a new state constitution, superseding all prior common-cause programs. In short, the social democracy phase of Chinese Communism was dead.

This constitution contained provisions for the establishment of a lifetime state chairmanship. Mao, who understood the people's desire for a robust, single-authority figure, positioned himself as that leader with his many writings and treatises on matters of life leadership. Mao had the security police and the military report directly to him through Politburo's Standing Committee as a final consolidation of power.

~

The practical, worldly Mao selected the well-liked, French-educated Zhou Enlai to be the country's first premier. Mao structured the premiership primarily to be a ceremonial role. But Mao knew the French-educated Zhou and his non-confrontational diplomatic manner would add legitimacy to his regime in those world capitals with the financial resources that could help rebuild the cash-strapped People's Republic. The elevation of the sophisticated Zhou gave many of China's self-exiled intellectual thought leaders a solid reason to return from Hong Kong. They believed they could contribute to re-establishing those elements of Chinese culture and tradition that would lift people's spirits and restore pride in China's unique history. I was among that naive group.

~

Zhou Enlai and I had a warm relationship since we both studied in France and came from similar family backgrounds. He was well aware I had used my composing and recital skills during the Sino-Japanese War to lift our soldiers' morale in battle and support the millions of displaced refugees.

In September 1954, I attended the First National Assembly, representing Tianjin city in Beijing. Premier Zhou Enlai asked me to consider moving my family and the Central Conservatory to Beijing. I expressed reluctance because of my disdain for politics, which indeed drove matters in Beijing. As it turned out, he would not take no for an answer.

Zhou and I met several times about moving to the Music Conservatory. He believed that the school, under my leadership, could recruit some of the finest young classical musicians in China and increase China's musical standing on the world cultural stage.

Finally, he made an offer that was so attractive it was impossible to refuse. Zhou was willing to raise my salary to be almost equivalent to Chairman Mao's, and Muli could pick and decorate any house she wanted in Beijing.

~

I met with Zhou shortly after our relocation. Mao Zedong entered. "Chairman, this is Ma Sicong, our gifted violinist who runs the Central Conservatory of Music."

"Ah, yes, the expensive one who studied in France." That's how I learned Mao was aware of my salary and was not particularly keen on my imperialist education.

"So Ma, is your music Western, or is it local Chinese with a heavy Hunan accent?" asked an emotionless Mao. I explained it was a merging of "the best elements of both."

I quickly learned Mao knew nothing about the creation of violin music; he stared blankly, then asked another question, "Does your art serve the masses?"

"I believe art serves the interested."

As I learned during the Cultural Revolution, those were not the answers Mao wanted to hear.

Chapter 24.

Best of Times

最好的时间

*Ma and Muli in their abundant garden
in a government-provided home in Beijing's best neighborhood*

As I look back over my roller-coaster life, I realize that the Beijing years were the best of times.

Muli and I selected a sprawling 200-year-old home that had been modernized, although the large front and backyards required tender loving care. As I worked hard establishing the Conservatory during the early months, Muli worked diligently with the gardeners to turn the grounds into a vibrant, beautiful garden filled with many varieties of fruit trees and colorful flowers. When the exterior work was complete, a news article entitled Ma Sicong's *Wonderful Spring Chords* read:

> "Foreign friends visiting Beijing love to be a guest at Ma's big courtyard home. The front yard is ripe with cypresses, pomegranates, magnolias, peaches, and the backyard with rows of lentils and gourds planted by hand each year. They say the harvests are so plentiful that every visitor leaves with an abundant harvest basket.
>
> "The living room, study, bedrooms, hallways, and even under the roof eaves are filled with potted plants of rubber trees, conifers, and camellias. And the sound of Ma's beautiful violin melody fills the air and can be heard from far, far away. Sometimes, he is joined by his beloved disciple, son Julon, now 11, who, like his father, played his first violin at seven. Father says his son 'has some talent.' Although others say he is far more talented.'"

~

Muli's tasteful decorating touch also turned the interior into a showcase for modern artworks. Many of the great Chinese painters of the day, such as Qi Baishi (*shee-by-shee*), Chang Dai-chien (*chang-ba-chen*), and Qian Songyan (*kin-sun-yen*), held exhibitions at the house. Qi, who would ultimately become Celia's godfather, gave Muli more than ten of his paintings in appreciation, including *Overflowing Wisteria*. His oversized masterpiece was eventually confiscated by the government and later auctioned for almost a hundred million dollars at today's exchange rate.

During my Beijing years, I also became an avid antique collector. Our recital schedule provided ample opportunity to acquire antiquities from all over China. Initially, Muli wanted to have them cleaned but stopped after a dealer explained, "Aging enhances beauty and value; it should not be disturbed."

Our home was also a magnet for culturally influential international guests—artists, painters, opera singers, and more—making Zhou feel the government was getting value received for their investment. One of Zhou Enlai's closest officials, Qiao Guanhau (*shoupa-hao*), and his wife, Kong Peng, frequently spent the weekend with us when no official government activities were scheduled.

~

I noticed Muli loved playing the role of the hostess, welcoming friends and guests with warmth and affection. One night, we were alone in the yard surrounded by the scent of fruit flowers. "I guess I would not have all these wonderful experiences if I had married my former fiancée." I nodded knowingly. I believe it was her way of saying, *I am willing to move on from your ill-conceived affair.*

~

Despite being part of China's cultural elite, I never stopped making music. My time in Beijing may have been one of my most musically productive periods, touring and completing 13 new compositions.

The tours were the first such events since the establishment of the People's Republic of China, and crowds were very curious. In Guangzhou alone, 13,000 people showed up for one concert, causing us to add two additional concerts

~

Soon, Mao created the Wu Fan movement to eliminate recalcitrant businesspeople and industrialists who participated in corrupt practices, tax evasion, bribery, and cheating on government contracts. While I supported the goals of the Wu Fun movement, I was never a member of the Communist Party, and I didn't involve myself in the school's daily operations. That role was filled by the vice president, who was a Party member. I focused on teaching music and expanding the school's curriculum. Much of my time was spent at home giving students lessons and monitoring their progress.

I was also responsible for creating a teacher's reeducation committee designed to self-examine capitalist thought and offer reforms consistent with Mao Zedong's callings. One summer, I and 35 other teachers labored with ordinary people to refine our thinking.

I suggested we work on the great Huai *(why)* River construction project in north Anhui *(ahh-way)*, where people worked ferociously to dredge the river and tame the flooding, which damaged the harvests and caused periodic famine.

We spent two months working side by side with the other workers, performing the hard labor of digging ditches and pushing mud-filled wheelbarrows. It was dirty, messy work, but I took pride in my job. I remember when Muli brought the children to visit; it took young Celia some time to recognize me since I was dark as coal in a t-shirt and shorts!

In the evenings, I would take out my violin and entertain the workers. They watched me and felt the emotion in my music. Soon, we were one—common people with a common purpose who worked hard and laughed out loud.

This experience became the motivation behind one of my compositions, the three-part *Huai River Cantana.*

In the first part, *The River,* I used a local folk melody to celebrate the people's work ethic. The second, *Spring Dance,* depicted the joys of folk dancers and their love for the land and life. The third part, *Lantern Festival Dance,* recalled the opening verse of the famous Chinese poem *Ode to the Lantern,* where the east wind blew open flowers in a thousand trees and brought down stars like rainfall at night.

~

In 1953, Premier Zhou requested a stage play to celebrate the 2,230th anniversary of our beloved patriotic poet and politician, Qu Yuan(*kee-yan*), known as China's first patriotic poet. Yuan had committed suicide rather than abandon his social principles. Qu Yuan's work, *A Poetic Drama,* was designed to celebrate Yuan's legendary social idealism and unwavering patriotism. Mao believed the popularity of such a drama would add credence to his position as the supreme leader of the Communist Party, who had fought and won the right to reward the peasant masses with a better life.

As head of the Music Academy, I was honored when Zhou asked me to compose the score, which many still regard as one of my most important works. The complex drama has seven movements: *Overture, Ode to Oranges, Drill Song, Spring Pleasing, Spirit-calling, Farewell,* and *Ode to Thunder and Lightning.* I made *Ode to Oranges* the underlying musical theme for the entire drama and used *Ode the Thunder and Lighting* to vividly portray Qu Yuan's suicidal rage at the climax.

~

Premier Zhou attended one of the later rehearsals. He congratulated all the players on a job well done, then he turned to me. "Ma, l feel your music maybe was so strong and loud in parts that the audience will not hear the lyrics. How do you feel?"

The room was dead silent; it was the first time anyone had ever challenged my musical judgment. I knew my reply required respect for Zhou's position.

"Perhaps you are right. My treatment may be a little heavy for this play. I'm accustomed to concerts where the music is always the priority."

During the next two days, I adjusted the music and conducted the orchestra to play lighter. The result? The music completely matched the play. Zhou was right!

As people stood and cheered during the opening night performance, Zhou, sitting in the first row, smiled and nodded at me as if to say, "I told you so."

Chapter 25.

My Favorite Composition

我最愛的作品

Ma and Gauguin shared a calling about nature.

As I worked to set Qu Yang's life to music, I became emotionally invested in his suicide and his relationship to China's beloved Chinese Dragon Boat Festival.

According to legend, Yuan entered the Miluo(*me-law*)River to drown himself because he realized his dream of a united motherland would never arrive. To save him, the nearby villagers feverously paddled to the middle of the river, beat their drums, splashed loudly with their paddles, and threw rice into the water to distract the evil spirits of death and reawaken his body. This ritual has remained part of my country's annual Chinese Dragon Boat Festival for the past 3,000 years.

~

Working on the score, I received a letter from a fan who had just listened to my *Pastoral for Violin*. The man said, "As soon as I heard your music on the radio, I recalled my youth in Yunnan Province, where the Nu River flowed." Attached to the letter was a folk song musical score. He said, "Perhaps it might provide some additional inspiration."

I played the score several times; the man was right. I imagined my musical sensibilities mesmerized by the spirit of the Mountain Elves conceived by Yuan. My composition, entitled *The Call of Mountain Forests,* called upon the listener to imagine the fresh aromas of nature one experiences when walking through a primal forest at daybreak.

I was pleased; I had captured the same spirit as one of my favorite works of art—French Impressionist Paul Gaugain's *The Call*. If you listen to my composition, you'll feel the presence of Yuan's Mountain Elf reaching out, not unlike the woman who extends her arm to call in Gaugain's painting. While many Chinese know *Mountain Forests* well, few know I believe it to be my favorite composition and my most important work. At the same time, I felt strongly that one of the greatest motivations for the artist is not current platitudes but the sense their work will be long remembered.

Over the years, *The Call of Mountain Forests* has been performed by some of the world's leading international orchestras from Russia,

Germany, France, and England, among others—when they toured China. I take great pleasure in that.

Chapter 26.

National Treasure

国寶

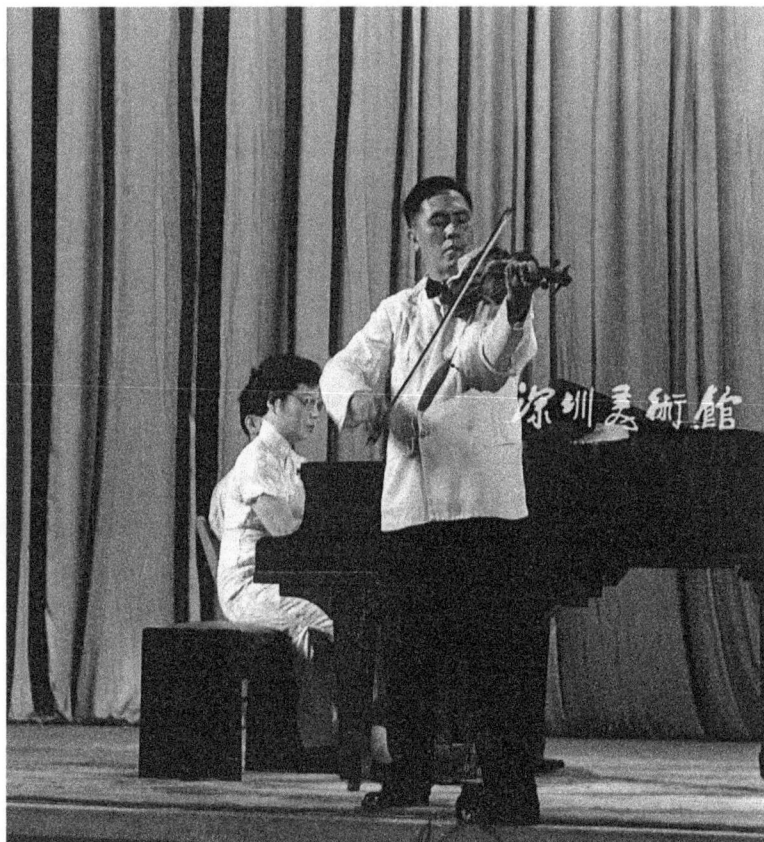

Ma traveled the world as China's Musical Ambassador

During the 1950s and early 1960s, I believed I was at my peak in composition, technique, and performance.

My music was filled with passion, love of the motherland, and the celebration of life. Even though my musical genres became more varied, my style became more nationalized, perhaps because of the influences of Mao and his teachings.

Thanks to the support of Chairman Mao and Premier Zhou, I also became one of China's leading musical ambassadors. Despite my lack of Communist Party membership and Mao's lingering concern that my music was not designed for the masses, I was invited to participate in many important state banquets in Peking and virtually all foreign cultural delegation events. While I generally thought of myself as a modest man who preferred to shun the limelight, I knew I was participating in the events of the privileged few.

In my unofficial capacity as a musical ambassador, I met many heads of state from Korea, Indonesia, Russia, Cambodia, Poland, and the Philippines, among others. I also had numerous conversations about the importance that music plays in celebrating a country's culture.

I was also in high demand as a performing artist, and to my surprise, I sold hundreds of thousands of record albums. One evening, Chairman Mao introduced me as "China's National Treasure." I was simply overwhelmed. I never imagined it!

~

During these heady times, there were also lighter moments. In the winter of 1953, I was dispatched to Korea and China's most famous operator singer, Mei Langang (*me-lan-ton*), well-known for his handsome appearance. A funny event happened when we visited Seoul in Korea. We were getting a haircut. A crowd had gathered outside to get a look at Mei. I left the barbershop first: the crowd swarmed, yelling, "Mei Lanfang! Mei Lanfang!" I quickly responded, "I am not Mei Lanfang! He is still inside!"

I tried to slip away, but the crowd only grew larger. The barber said, "Mr. Mei Lanfang, can you please say something to your fans."

Outside, the crowd grew even more significant. I said to the barber, "I am not Mei Lanfang." The barber still did not believe me, so it was simpler to pretend I was Mei Lanfang and greet the fans. When Mei finally came outside, he was surprised to find no fans.

~

In February 1956, the King of Cambodia, Norodom Sihanouk, made his first visit to China. Zhou Enlai gave him a warm reception, and they signed a friendship treaty in which China promised $40 million (U.S. dollars) in economic aid to Cambodia.

I was asked to perform after dinner. Later, the king and I began to chat informally. Sihanouk was an intelligent, gentle person with an extraordinary interest in classical music. Premier Zhou could see my chemistry with the new king. He called over his French-educated Minister of Foreign Affairs, Chen Yi. "Chen, how is it we *all* went to France to study, and Ma learned much, but we did not learn anything?"

~

In March 1956, I was invited to Poland for the Chopin International Piano International Competition. A gifted, young Chinese pianist, Fou Ts'ong (*doe-foo*), was also invited. It was the first time China had a judge on the jury and a musician in this competition. The judges were required to follow specific uniform rules to produce scores for each participant. But national pride took over; each judge wished their country's candidate to win and gave their competitors deductions for the slightest fundamental mistake.

As a result, no competitor stood out during the first round of the competition. Fou was nervous and slow; he placed sixth. At the break, I explained his weaknesses. Some judges were surprised by Fou's improvements and poetic expression of Chopin's unique music during the second round. The judges eliminated several competitors, and Fou placed third.

But Fou did win the Mazuka Award, given to the pianist who best represented Chopin's most personal instinct, individuality, and inner feeling. Previously, only Polish and Slavic artists had won this award. No Asian had ever come close.

When we returned home, I convinced Premier Zhou that Fou should hold a public recital sponsored by the government. Zhou wanted to know why. I explained, "Showcasing Fou's talent to other young musicians in China will benefit commitment to the state." Months later, Fou performed in front of thousands of young Chinese pianists.

~

In the middle of my travel and tours, Chairman Mao launched two initiatives: the Anti-Rightist Campaign and the Great Leap Forward. The former campaign was created to purge all Rightists within the Communist Party of China and abroad. I found the definition of rightists confusing but took it to mean those intellectuals who appeared to favor capitalism and were against collectivization.

The Great Leap Forward, which continued well into the 1960s, was an economic and social campaign designed to convert China's agrarian economy into a communist society filled with abundance by forming people's communes. It quickly became apparent the Great Leap Forward was a failure; there were no surpluses, leaving farmers and families to starve. Higher officials did not dare to report the economic disaster caused by these policies, blaming bad weather for the decline in food output, and took little or no action. It would be years later when I learned that more than 500,000 intellectuals had been murdered, and 25-40 million workers died in the Great Chinese Famine.

~

I was troubled by the Chairman's latest movements, especially as I learned so many friends and relatives had become victims. Since my music remained in high demand, I turned a blind eye. It is a mistake I've never forgotten! Further, on many occasions when the Chairman and I met, I found him a brilliant man who had the wisdom to love poetry and the arts. Even when we had different opinions on matters, I found him able to reach mutual understandings. I remember one particular debate over tea. Chairman Mao said, "I believe music has to be immediately loved by the masses."

I replied, "I disagree. Sometimes music will take years for the masses to understand. That does not make it any less valuable."

Mao said, "You are right."

Despite my cordial relationship with the Chairman, many music critiques started to appear in the authoritative *People's Music Journal*.

"Ma Sicong's music is full of dreaming, sweetness, aesthetics. Of course, laboring masses need beauty, but the spirit of the Great Leap Forward is socialism, communism—the spirit of proletariat selflessness. Ma Sicong's *Ave Maria*-style music is one hundred thousand miles different from that spirit."

As I learned, these criticisms were just preludes to the disastrous Cultural Revolution, known formally as the Great Proletarian Cultural Revolution.

~

In September 1957, the government held a Higher Education Teachers Conference. I was allowed to speak about whatever was on my mind. By this time in China, when artists spoke freely, they were labeled "outdated rightists," non-Communist Party followers who wished to spread their poisonous thinking. An intellectual, labeled as such, stood the risk of being ostracized by his peers and could lose their social status or, worse yet, lose their job. At a minimum, they could face the need for "re-education."

Not yet realizing the full political impact of my opinions, I chose observations on the state of music and titled my remarks, *A Hundred Flowers Bloom, A Hundred Schools of Thought Contend.*

"Today, in China, our most serious problem is that our creative works have become formula and routine. There are too many rules in creating music. For example, if we only allow march music for the masses to be developed, other types of music will be ignored.

"Songs expressing emotion will be frowned upon, and people will be afraid to write and sing such music. In reality, people love good, touching music that can express emotions in their hearts. For an extended period, there was a trend not to promote European-style music. The logic behind this trend was that the masses dislike this type of music. I am happy to report, there are some improvements in this aspect of our music, although the pace may be too slow for my taste."

"About music critics. Most feel obligated to offer lots of criticisms, but very few offer encouragement. Further, their judgments are narrow, shallow, and short-sighted. They refuse to pay attention and give credit to new, fresh creations—critics should be careful not to ruin these fragile new seedlings.

"I also believe we should be cautious of critic-controlled publications. They should be careful not to allow false evidence or rude language against those who dissent. I think authoritative music publications have limited honest debate. 'A Hundred Schools of Thought Contend' should allow different views to prevail openly and candidly, rather than use their platform to allow one side to silence the other side."

~

Despite being increasingly labeled a rightist, Premier Zhou still wanted me to tour out of step with current musical trends and beliefs. He knew I could be his musical ambassador because I was not a politician with an appetite for power. The eight-month tour across China ended with four sold-out concerts in Peking. (Peking did not become Beijing until 1979). Fortunately, people also seemed more curious about my newly acquired violin than about my quasi-political music musings. The music journal *Capital Paper* published an article entitled *A Priceless Old Violin*, which did an excellent job of illustrating the subtleties of my instrument.

"Ma's violin was made more than 300 years ago by the Italian master violin maker Andrea Amati. Ma's violin is a rare, priceless masterpiece, lighter than a handful of cotton. A large part of varnish on the violin head and body is worn with age, but, miraculously, the fish pattern on the Maplewood still sparkles. When one looks closely at the violin's F-holes, one will see the name and ages of the violin owners in Italian."

I was pleased with the newspaper article, but for me, the instrument was all about the soft, loud, clear sound it created. When I played my new, 300-year-old violin at the grand hall in Guangzhou for the first time, every one of the 5,000 people in the audience could hear clearly without the need for a microphone.

~

After the tour, I remained steadfast in my music beliefs, and there were no overt rumblings of dissatisfaction from Chairman Mao. My most beloved composition—*Nostalgia*—continued to be broadcast on Chinese radio every morning.

My conclusion? I remained in high regard given my close relationship with Premier Zhou and highly visible position as one of China's music thought-leaders.

I was wrong. Someone betrayed me!

~

During her early school days, we noticed first daughter Bixue was unlike her mild-mannered little sister Celia—Bixue insisted on always taking the lead. She was quite the accomplished pianist, easily qualified to enter the Central Conservatory of Music, and lived with grandma Huang in Shanghai. During that period, we rarely communicated and offered little parental advice. Muli and I learned from grandma that Bixue had decided to live at the school dormitory to "better participate in the thoughts of the younger generation."

During her freshman year in 1957, Chairman Mao Ma launched his Anti-rightest campaign. Bixue jumped at the opportunity to become a devoted Chinese Communist Party member, follow the party doctrine religiously, and ignore the reality that hundreds of thousands of intellectuals were being sentenced to hard labor and executed, including a number of my friends and acquaintances.

When Bixue did visit home, our conversations were spirited. She challenged my decision not to become a member of the Communist Party. I told her I was simply a musician who dreamed of a day when the People's Republic of China would offer opportunities to everyone and welcome free thought.

She bristled at my explanation. "You are more than a musician. You are a person of great influence!" Each subsequent visit brought more challenging questions.

"Why inject bourgeois West traditions into our Eastern music?" "Why was grandfather a revolutionary?"

"Why didn't Chiang Kai-shek believe all peasants deserve a better life like Chairman Mao?"

Her questions cut deeply. It was apparent someone had re-educated in ways I loathed.

But Bixue was family; I felt the need to be open and honest. One day, my friends at the party approached me. They suggested I be careful what I say to my daughter because they had seen reports where things I had said could leave me in political disfavor. From that moment forward, Bixue and I never spoke about social and political matters.

When Bixue graduated, she decided to live in Beijing, teach at the conservatory, and cut off all communications with Muli and me. I was now a father with one daughter and one son.

Chapter 27.

My First Tatzepao

我的第一個大字報

Large posters with large letters were used to confess crimes

Initially, I had no idea how far the latest Cultural Revolution would go. Conditions were tense, but I recalled far more unsettling times in China. Under Mao, there had already been many short-lived thought-reform campaigns, including Three Anti-Five Anti, the Great Leap Forward, and the Anti-Rightists, among others. Besides having lived through revolutions, civil wars, and my father's assassination, I knew China was never an easy place to live—that was a fact of life.

The difference this time was that I was being attacked personally. Big character posters called *tatzepao (taa-so-pow)* had been put up at the Music Academy. Scrawled on newspaper or butcher paper, they carried news, accusations, confessions, announcements, or praise for Chairman Mao. Such posters became the hallmark of the Cultural Revolution.

A friend suggested that my wisest move would be to write self-criticism before things went any further. My wife and daughter agreed. I hesitated; I had nothing to confess. Besides, I was not too fond of the idea of putting myself forward, but protecting my family and my professional reputation, shattered as it was, was paramount.

Reluctantly, I agreed, and Celia wrote a statement for me. It said that I supported the Cultural Revolution enthusiastically and, though I did not admit to any wrongdoing, I was willing to accept reform. We bought three pieces of yellow paper and made the statement into *a* tatzepao entitled *My Determination*, and I took it to the Academy.

At this point, the Red Guards did not yet exist as they would come to be known. They called themselves "revolutionary teachers and students," and they were starting to disrupt the administration of the Music Academy. Chao Feng, a party member and vice president of the Music Academy, had been *de facto* school boss since 1957. When I arrived with my tatzepao, Chao would not let me post it. Soon, he was replaced by an army officer named Wang, who I realized knew nothing about music. Wang quickly fell into disgrace. His crime? He tried to call the police to break up a fight between two groups of revolutionary students. He was reprimanded for not seizing control of the Academy and was banished into the hands of a work team sent by the Ministry of Culture. These changes were unimportant in themselves but showed the sort of progressive anarchy that marked the Cultural Revolution. It was never easy to tell who was in charge. Often no one was.

~

With Chao Feng and Wang out, I was again directed to post my *tatzepao*. The night I went to school, I had to read my post to those who had publicly ridiculed me. I knew all of my accusers; they were embarrassed for their actions, but the Revolution forced people close to you to write terrible things. They also composed posters that criticized my music as bourgeois and said that the family lived too comfortable a life in "a fairy tale existence far from the real world with a car, a cook, an elegant chicken coop, and too many cats." Actually, we had only one cat, which the Red Guards later killed and ate.

As I was preparing to go home, a student from the high school affiliated with the Academy insisted that I accompany him to his school. Instead, he led me to an angry group of teenagers who surrounded me and began shouting about a piece of music I had written. The ignorant young people misunderstood the intent of the composition. It was an elegy to a heroic district party secretary named Caho Yu-lu, who had died in the service of his peasant constituents. It was an example of patriotic commitment. I wrote this kind of music from time to time just to stay out of trouble, though in this case, I did admire the man.

For some reason, the teenagers were infuriated, "Why did you make the music so sad? You don't deserve to be a follower of Caho Yu-lu." Then they sent me home with a bundle of new tatzepao that I was supposed to hang up outside my house and read. I put them away in a storeroom, instead.

Several days later, a call came from the Music Academy telling me to report. I didn't take the call, and I didn't go. The next day, I decided it would probably be wiser to comply. I phoned for my car, which was kept at the school. "No," my chauffeur said to me, "Now the Cultural Revolution is on; you can't use the car. Take the bus."

~

When I got to school, I was forced to stand around the office for hours. Old friends would look at me, but nobody even said hello. I asked a man in a work team who was, at that time, running the school what I should do. "Go into the auditorium," he pointed. "They are waiting for you."

I walked out into a mob of several hundred growling students. "Down with bourgeois authority!" Down with this and that, and after every slogan, some people would yell "Mao Tse-tung wansui [long live our leader]." One fellow accidentally shouted my Chinese name by mistake, "Ma T'set'sung." They pushed me to the back, and then someone threw a satchel at me. Before long, more satchels and pens and such were thrown at me. I could do nothing but stand there. The entire scene felt unreal and somewhat ridiculous; I knew it was unlikely everyone believed all the slogans they were shouting.

Finally, the humiliation was over. I was instructed to get on a bus and go home. As I waited on the corner, a student asked me pleasantly, "What did you feel about the mass criticism today?"

I thought to myself, what an ignorant question! I replied, "It was very educational."

Chapter 28.

Study Training

訓練学習

Brainwashing young students and aging adults was called study training

Not long after the auditorium incident, 17 of us were called to the school and advised that we had been selected for study training. I realized I was no longer in favor. My fall from grace had been swift and deep.

When I arrived, I met various Music Academy professors and administrators, including Vice President Chao Feng, who looked as though he had not slept for days. Many of the educators were Party members. We were bused to the Socialist Institute, formerly a university for training Communist cadres in Marxist philosophy; it was now rumored to be a concentration camp for intellectuals and prominent cultural figures.

Everybody involved in cultural affairs was there: artists, actors, musicians, motion picture directors, writers, cultural officials, and professors from the Fine Arts Academy and the Motion Picture Academy. There must have been 500 of us; my roommate was Abing, China's most famous erh-hu (Chinese violin) player.

I spent 50 days at the Institute, from the middle of June to the beginning of August. It was incredibly tedious but not brutal. Organized into brigades and supervised by army officers, we were put to work reading endless documents and holding worthless discussion meetings. When we had any free time, we were supposed to write new tatepazos criticizing ourselves and the other misguided cliques within the Party.

One day, we received extraordinary news: Chou Yang (*chow-yan*), the influential deputy director of the Department of Culture and Propaganda of the Communist Party Central Committee, had fallen. For years, he had been our direct superior and had played a leading role in many of Chairman Mao's purges. From him had emanated rulings on all sorts of cultural matters, including what Western Music might be performed in China. Except for a short period in 1962, Debussy and Ravel were prohibited, along with most twentieth-century composers. Beethoven, Brahms, Schubert, and other classical composers were permissible until the general ban on Western music began in 1963.

Yang had always been considered the ideal representative of the thoughts of Mao Zedong. Now we were told, by the vice-minister who succeeded him, that Chou Yang's views were "smelly, long and deep." He was now the "Number One Demon in the Kingdom of Hell."

I suppose he might have spent time with us in study training, but he was in the hospital dying from lung cancer!

No one dared to talk about the arbitrariness of these changes. We were taught to distrust each other. We all believed that the wrong word about intimate matters was too dangerous. Others might be spies. Many of the brightest minds in China were relegated to talking about the weather while society was being shaken to its very foundation.

~

When my group arrived at the Socialist Institute, we were told that our study would last from eight months to a year, depending upon how malleable we were. Somehow, we kept thinking up new subjects for the *tatzepao*. They got very detailed and personal. I wasn't attacked very often, except by some department heads who felt they had to say something. The most specific charges leveled at me were in a *tatzepao* written by my former chauffeur at the Music Academy. He claimed I had mistreated him. To live at my house, he said he was forced to obey many unreasonable rules, such as no spitting on the floors, no coughing, no talking in a loud voice, and his children were not allowed to cry. Finally, I had made him work so hard that he got sick.

Another tatzepao, from a former cook, said my daughter had sent him out for ice cream in the rain, after which he became ill and had to go to the hospital.

~

According to the Party, the Ministry of Culture dispatched speakers to give us periodic news from the outside. There were hair-raising reports about Yang and his bloodthirsty henchmen with rifles and artillery, surrounding the central district in Peking where Mao and the other leaders lived.

We, of course, knew little about what was going on, other than student excitement for the Cultural Revolution. At Tsing Hua University in Peking, the first Red Guard units had been formed. In other schools across China, similar misguided groups had formed that quickly created a near state of turmoil.

We observed that excitement and turmoil firsthand when several Music Academy teachers and I were forced to watch two hideous meetings against Chao Feng. Chao tried to confess his sins while standing on a large platform in the auditorium, but he was shouted down by the students and workers who swore at him and insulted him, calling him a dog.

The first meeting lasted two hours, the second eight! The accusations against Chao were bizarre—that he had secret dealings with the British in Hong Kong, abused workers and stolen furniture from the school, and took a picture showing him with Chairman Mao. The violence and hysteria of the crowd were out of all proportion to the near-frivolity of the charges. I found it terrifying. I also felt sad for my homeland, which had been allowed to fall into anarchy. I thought to myself, what happened to the Chairman Mao I knew? Who placed this demon of perverted thought in his place? How could this demon let so many of his country die to achieve his misguided objectives?

Despite being surrounded by sheer madness, we were left relatively unscathed for a while. It was rumored that the Socialist Institute was the idea of Liu Shao-ch'l *(yu-sha-pe)*, president of China, who wanted to give China's thought and cultural leaders some form of protection from the Red Guards. He placed us in the army's hands, which, for all their intellectual shortcomings, were at least disciplined. However, at the beginning of August, Liu—who once stood only third in power to Chairman Mao and Premier Zhou—lost power. In late 1969, he died of a mysterious illness and was cremated the next day. His children did not learn of his death until 1972.

To this day, there is no doubt that Liu had a falling out with his superiors and was probably murdered. No one will ever know for sure. But the practical consequence of his fall from grace had terrible implications on me—I was returned to the increasingly hostile masses of Red Guards.

Chapter 29.

Dunce Cap

戴高帽

Ma and fellow intellections publicly humiliated and paraded

One evening, trucks marked Hei-ban chuanche'e (special truck for the Black Gang) came to the Motion Picture Institute, picked up all the members, and took them away. I never saw them again. The following day, the rest of us climbed into a similar truck and were returned to the Music Academy.

As we entered the gate, we were greeted by a large crowd of students, workers, soldiers, and even children. We were prodded off the truck like cows. Without warning, someone dumped a bucket of paste on my head and rammed a tall dunce cap labeled "cow demon" on my head. A cardboard plaque around my neck said, "Ma Sicong, agent of the bourgeois opposition." Later, another sign that called me a "vampire" was added. Finally, they gave each of us a death bell —a copper basin with a stick to beat it. Chao Feng, identified as the Boss of the Black Gang, was also forced to wear a heavy sheepskin wrap. The day was as hot as Peking can be, 100+ degrees.

Our assailants acted as if they had gone crazy. We were paraded across the campus. All the way, hordes of young people shouted slogans, hit us with sticks, and spit on us, especially the children. I even recognized the distorted faces of some of my students in the crowd.

Finally, they made us bow our heads and form two rows on the stage. Those of us in the Black Gang whose crimes were considered most serious were placed in the first row; the lesser demons were in the second row because they had merely said something wrong. Among them was the pianist Liu Shih-k'un, the runner-up to Van Cliburn in the world-famous Moscow piano competition nine years earlier.

Weeks later, Liu protested about the living conditions in Study School. The Red Guards dragged him out of his room and smashed his wrists so viciously that he was never able to play the piano again.

~

As it turned out, these events were only the *beginning* of a month of constant degradation and harassment.

That first day, we were kept on public display for several hours and then taken to a row of small, low buildings at the rear of the school grounds, which had been used to store pianos. I was given a tiny room in one of these, scarcely larger than the bed that stood in it. Only six of us had such separate rooms—the four department heads, Chao and myself. The others shared rooms.

There was no advantage to having a separate room because one wall was nearly all glass. The guards could come and look at me anytime they wanted. I was told, "Since you are an animal, you should be displayed like an animal." On the walls of my room were signs such as "Down with Vampires!" and "If you are not honest, we will crush your dog's head." The entrance to my building also had a sign: "Nests of Devils and Demons."

Despite the ongoing hostility, we had a routine. Every morning, we got up at 6:00 A.M., studied *Mao's Selected Works* or read Party newspaper editorials for half an hour, ate breakfast, and then labored from 8:00 A.M. to noon. It was primarily dirty work. We cleaned latrines, chopped firewood, and did a good bit of pointless labor, such as making big piles of scattered stones and shifting the entire contents of one building to another. Our guards would frequently ask us, "How was your work? Did you work well?"

All afternoon and in the evening, we had to compose self-criticisms full of phrases like "We are Chao Feng's bourgeois black gangsters," "We are objects for reform and struggle," and "We have to accept the supervision of the masses." These were turned over daily to our captors.

Every morning and evening, we had to sing together—and sometimes alone—a disgusting song composed by the son of the professor of conducting. It was called *The Howl of the Black Gangsters*.

> I am a cow-headed monster,
> I have sinned, I have sinned.
> I must come under the people's dictatorship
> Because I am an enemy of the people.
> I must be very frank,
> If I am not, smash me to bits!

The song ended on the seventh chord crescendo to make it sound repulsive.

None of this was pleasant, but the most nerve-wracking thing was the random harassment. At any time, the Red Guards could order us out of our rooms. "Come out!" they would say, "Bow your head!" Because I had been labeled a vampire for ill-treating workers

—namely my chauffeur—they would force me to recite my crimes over and over.

The misguided children were the fiercest, most vicious of all. The revolutionary brainwashing had turned them into little demons. They made me crawl on my hands and knees. They tore up my room on several occasions, pulled the bedding apart, and scattered my books. One boy took my quilt and threw it on the roof, remarking, "So long as there is Mao's revolution, no action we take is a crime."

These Red Guards had no leaders, and we were fair game for any of them. It was anarchy. Sometimes they would order us to face a wall and then forget about us. Other times, we were forced to stand in the hot sun for hours with our heads deeply bowed.

One night I was asleep in my room when there was a terrible banging on the door. Two Red Guards burst in, a boy and a girl, no more than 14 years old, and demanded, "Stand up!" I struggled to my feet. "Faster," they shouted. The boy took off his belt and started to whip me while the girl laughed and spit in my face. I was bloodied but not severely injured.

On another occasion, they beat Chao Feng in the next room so severely that he fell to the ground, and they left him in a pool of his blood. I heard him wincing in pain. I tried to open my door, but it was locked.

~

I saw many other inhumane acts, but I will spare the reader many of those things, although I will never forget. But I think it's important to understand what unspeakable things man can do to a man!

The son of one of the imprisoned department heads got into a fight with Red Guards, who had come to vandalize his father's home. The enraged boy pulled a knife and tried to stab a Red Guard. They hauled him off to the police.

The Red Guards returned to the Academy and told the man, "Your son's foolish choice is about to cause you great pain." The man praised his son, and then the Guards beat him into a bloody pulp.

Soon, there came a new tapzepao that said, "If you harm one hair of a Red Guard, you will be smashed up."

A day later, an important struggle meeting (public humiliation and torture session) was held outdoors. A platform had been established at one side of a large courtyard for the bloodied department head and his accusers. Many people came forward out of the crowd to level accusations. The rest of us were ordered to squat in the sun and watch.

Red Guards dragged four or five men and women—friends who had defended the man—up to the platform and swore at them. Then a Guard took a large leather whip and began beating them. The department head was beaten most savagely of all. Somebody screamed, "You see! Look what happens to those who oppose." The poor man lay in the sun for hours before he died.

Later that same evening, the Red Guards were invited to beat us, too, on the pretext that we were not bowing low enough. I didn't resist. The Guard took off his thick leather belt with a heavy metal bucket and began to smash it against my head. I covered my head with my hands, which only made the Guards more vicious. When they finished, my bruised body lay battered on the floor; I vowed if I ever awoke from this nightmare, I promised I would never return to my homeland as long as Mao's madness continued.

Chapter 30.

Red Guard Frenzy

疯狂的紅衛兵

Vicious Red Guards abused and killed the innocent

After my beatings, physical violence inexplicably slacked off at the Academy. Elsewhere in the city, however, the atrocities accelerated. Students at one high school beat to death every one of their teachers. The woman who lived next door to us in the west city was accused of having a radio transmitter and sending messages to Chiang Kai-shek. Red Guards pulled her from her house into the street and killed her. People spoke of heaps of unburied bodies rotting in the mortuaries.

Fear of this unpredictable violence caused my family to flee from Peking. Later, my daughter Celia told me that a friend brought word of seeing me covered in paste and foul tatzepao at the Academy. He told Celia it was "only a matter of time" before a team of students and Guards would be coming to seize her and her mother.

Muli and Celia made plans to leave. They moved some things— including my recent unpublished compositions—14 significant works —to friends' houses and sold other belongings to the second-hand store to raise some travel monies.

Sure enough, that same night, a gang from the Academy arrived. Muli hid in the chicken coop in the back garden, but the students dragged her out. They also caught Celia. More than half of the students were my daughter's former classmates. Their leader, whom she had known as a tall, gentle, naive cello student nicknamed "Camel," brutally recounted their crimes.

Outside, children filling the streets clamored to be allowed to beat the "criminals." Students from the Academy demanded newspaper, brushes, and ink and used them to produce tatzepao posted all over the house. They vowed to return so they could attach new tatzepao to my wife and daughter personally. Before dawn, my wife and children (Julon was away at class during the earlier visit that evening) dressed themselves in poor, ragged clothes and fled by bus to a city in central China where some friends lived. I, of course, knew nothing of this. They did not need approved papers to travel, only money to buy tickets.

I am sure that if my son and daughter had not dropped out of school several years before to study at home, they would have been forced to become Red Guards. Young people who refused to join invited trouble.

Celia told me later that there had been long, exhausting debates, sometimes hysterical, among Music Academy students. In the end, one-third of the extremists, who accepted guidance from the Central Party authorities, won out over the two-thirds of the student body who believed more new purges would destroy the school. This same kind of argument took place in many colleges, but the results were always the same. It always ended badly for the losers, who refused to cooperate.

~

As we moved into autumn, conditions changed. Tens of thousands of Red Guards from other parts of China swarmed into Peking and lived in the schools. It was an unsavory mess—unkept Red Guards were everywhere. They had no real organization or discipline; they simply went from city to city, raising the Red Flag. While the streets remained dangerous, there were no longer guards at the Academy doors, and nobody paid much attention to whether we were studying and writing confessions on schedule. The man in charge of us was not too bright, and I think he got bored with the intellectually tedious Marxist philosophy.

A few months later, we were permitted to spend parts of weekends at home and, by November, we could go home every night, returning to school for study and labor on weekdays. This treatment reflected both the confusion brought on by the Red Guard influx and the fact that attention was shifting from *cultural criminals* to *corrupt government officials*.

~

I was happy to get home, but it looked nothing like the pleasant place I had known before. My family was gone. All my books, records, and other belongings and had been confiscated or smashed. Two workers and their families had taken over part of the house, and the rest was filled with sixty or so Red Guards who slept in our former living room and my daughter's room, laid out like cordwood!

I stayed in the room that had been my study. Only two books, both translations, had been inadvertently left by the marauders. One was *The Call of the Wild* by Jack London, and the other was about Greek mythology. I was only allowed to read the London book once, but it seemed that the dog's life was much like mine.

Muli and Celia desperately wanted to see me. I felt the same. We had been apart far too long. They traveled north on the train to Peking, which was packed to overflow. They were questioned very closely by the Red Guards and nearly seized. Celia talked roughly, which convinced them that she and my wife were merely ignorant, poor peasants traveling to see her grandmother. When they got to Peking, they had planned to stay with friends, but because of the presence of Red Guards, no one dared take them in, so they returned to the station and hid in the crowd for several hours before boarding another train heading south.

Two weeks later, Celia traveled to Peking alone. We met at the home of a friend far out in the southern suburbs, where we spoke in a small, dark, closet-like room off the yard for hours while my friend watched the door. Celia bought me a piece of mooncake. After devouring every last crumb, I said, "Celia, this is the best tasting mooncake I have ever eaten!"

Shortly after Celia left, a team of Red Guards from the Music Academy arrived, seeking to capture and humiliate her. My friend said he knew nothing. That's when I decided to maintain a low profile in the small coastal city by attending school on a worn, used bicycle. Eventually, Red Guard surveillance relaxed, and it again appeared to be safe to communicate in letters. I wrote Celia she should not be attempting to visit; it was still too dangerous.

But Celia had Muli's determined spirit. Soon she appeared in the middle of the night at our house. She warned, "There is much speculation in our hometown about your whereabouts." Ceclia told stories about how people were trying to escape from China—some walked while others went by boat, but she had few details. The idea struck me like a thunderbolt—I should arrange a daring escape plan.

Still, I had not quite prepared myself for such a step. I was torn. China was my roots: my parent's homeland and that of my grandparents. But Chairman Mao had changed my love, my patriotism, to fear for the future.

My music, which had caused my celebrity, could also be my downfall. I was quickly recognized. It was just a matter of time before I was caught trying to escape, classified as a t'do ping (a deserter), and turned into another nameless body in another mass grave. Even if I arranged a family escape plan, there still was a good chance of failure.

Regardless of the odds, I owed my family the opportunity for a better life. So Celia and I fled by bus and train to meet Muli and Julon at the far end of a train platform. The night before we left, I was filled with doubt and worry. An ancient Chinese proverb replayed in my head: "I was standing with my back to the water."

~

Fortunately, Muli's mother, living in Shanghai, had connections and a plan for us to escape to Hong Kong. She pleaded in her note: "Under no circumstances should you deviate from the plan; there will be no second chance."

Celia stood in line for half the night at Ch'ien Men Station until she finally secured train tickets. She carried a few things for safekeeping, particularly my violin, and had made two bundles tied with rope. Unfortunately, my new compositions had to be abandoned.

I followed my routine. I reported to the school for morning labor —cleaning latrines—then said I was ill and had to go to the clinic. Once out of sight, I dressed all in dark blue workman clothes and then added an extra disguise: a standard surgical-type gauze mask over my mouth, which many people in China wore to ward off colds and other sicknesses, such as encephalitis.

It was a bitterly cold Tuesday night when we met at a temporary station outside the His Chih Gate, boarded an express bus, and left Peking for good. There had been a few frightening moments because the bus ran late, but fortunately, so did the connecting train. For the first time in months, my mind was somewhat at ease.

Celia and I found my son Julon staying with family friends in the city's center near the coast. My wife was in a tiny village in the same region. To get there, you had to take a train, then a bus, cross a river by boat, and finally walk. The trip took most of the day, and it was suppertime when we arrived. My wife was eating alone in the half-darkness. She had no idea I was coming, so it was quite a shock.

We were finally together again. Our adventure to an unknown destination was about to continue.

Chapter 31.

Goodbye Mao

再見老毛

The badge of Mao people wore to demonstrate loyalty

We stayed in the village during the next few weeks waiting for word about what was next in the city.

An old friend in the city got in touch with a woman who knew of a boat captain. Although he had no boat of his own—his boatyard had been nationalized in 1950—the man was in a position to steal one. He planned to do so in a few weeks. The woman knew nothing more but was willing to put us into contact with the boat captain's son.

When I spoke to the son, he was unsure if there would be enough room for all of us, or any of us, for that matter; he would let us know. The price per head would be the equivalent of US $1,500.

As Celia said, this city was indeed full of escape talk. Julon had heard of boys trying to escape as many as eight times, suffering a few months of hard labor each time they were caught. It would be much different if we were captured because my escape could be a worldwide embarrassment to Chairman Mao. As all Chinese know, a leader never wishes to be embarrassed in public.

Time was going fast, and I was getting worried. The Red Guards were everywhere, and I was concerned the village was becoming hard to hide because it was so small. There were open fights between the Red Guards and the workers in the streets and a growing number of terrible atrocities, further increasing the Red Guard presence.

The captain's son and I met again; he said we could join them on the boat, assuming we could prove we weren't being followed. "If I find anyone even trying to follow, the deal is off." He also assured me that the boat was fast enough to get away from patrol vessels and had a very shallow draft, so it could easily cross the sandbars.

~

A day or two later, word came that the arrangements had fallen through. We sent Celia to the city to find out what had gone wrong. She reported the women who set up the meetings had decided it was too dangerous to help us arrange another meeting with the boat people. "Things are getting better in Peking," the woman insisted, as she pointed to my records, which were back on sale in city shops.

As far as I was concerned, this was a disaster. I imagined government officials placed the records on sale to lure me into a sense of safety. I knew it was too late to go back, and the boat was due to leave in a day or two, with or without us. Our only hope was a faint one: find the woman who knew the boatman's son.

Celia remembered the street, but not the house where the woman lived. She had been there once. Perhaps she could find it again. We rode a bus, passing over a bridge. The street must have had 200 numbers. We walked up and down several times, staring at the fronts of the buildings in the faint light of the streetlamps. We knocked on a number of the wrong doors.

Suddenly, Celia remembered the name of the woman's uncle, Li Dehong. The next time we knocked, we asked for Li Dehong. "Not here, but next store." Once again, we were in touch. The next afternoon, Celia and I met the boatman's son at the teahouse in the park.

He said there was still room for us on the boat. I suspect space may have already been allocated, but the boatman and his son were extremely fond of violin music. When they learned who I was, they were willing to take us without an outside guarantee for the money.

We waited another week to set the day set for sailing. My family split up, staying in different places in the city. I went out as little as possible because Red Guards were parading everywhere. Finally, on the appointed night, we took a bus out of the city. We got off the bus an hour later and walked down a small road, flanked by the river on one side and fields on the other. We carried nothing—my only baggage, my violin, had been sent ahead. The sun was well down, but the sky was still light. We noticed two people standing near the road. They looked at us as we passed. I became increasingly nervous, but they didn't stop us.

The plan was to meet the boatman's son and his brother where the river ran into a broad estuary. They would be dressed as hunters, with big hats and shotguns, and pretend to be shooting birds. Their guns and flashlights would be used to signal the boat, which would be waiting offshore for us to arrive in a small rowboat. This time, however, they motioned for us to go back. They were suspicious of the two people standing by the roadway, who turned out to be workers from a nearby factory.

~

Three days later, on a rainy night, we tried a second time. The narrow road was very muddy. But once again, we had to go back. The boat captain could not steal the engine key because of a meeting in progress at the shipyard.

We were seven or eight days into the lunar month, and the moonlight was increasing in brilliance. Another two days and the moon would be too bright to travel safely, and we'd have to wait another sixteen days for it to wane sufficiently. I felt the tension. There was nothing to do but wait and talk and hope. Julon and I practiced diving into a shoebox-sized hideout that our host had prepared if Red Guards came.

On the last possible day, we again went to the river and huddled under a tree. The night light was bright, and there was a slight wind blowing. The river had the fresh, clean smell of winter water. We had to wait a long time for darkness to descend, but the signal finally came.

We all ran as fast as we could over the rough sandy rise between us and the open shore. Our boat had almost beached. Someone whispered," Quick," and we piled in. There were 13 people, enough to weigh the boat dangerously. There could have been two or three inches of freeboard above the waterline. Thank heaven, the waves were only ripples.

Offshore in the blackness, the larger vessel sputtered, *phut, phut, phut.* We drew up to the ship and scrambled aboard like crabs. At first, we all crowded into the small forward cabin, but the boat captain ordered my family and two others to go to the stern for better balance. We lay down side by side, closely huddled together against the cold wind.

I had been told we would travel about twelve li per hour (four miles), but it turned out that the best we could do was two miles an hour, so it would take twice as long as planned to get past the three-mile limit. En route, we had to negotiate several customs checkpoints. Fortunately, the captain knew the officials handling these posts were in the process of being replaced, having been labeled as "politically unreliable" members of the Cultural Revolution. Hence, the odds of getting to safety were in our favor.

As we passed the last checkpoint, a bright light suddenly fell on us, which seemed to come from everywhere at once. A boat cautiously approached our stern. It was only 50 feet away. Thinking that we had been discovered, our captain abruptly steered off to the right. The boat turned out to be a big, slow freighter and did not follow us. No sooner had we turned into the new course, another light flared; this one came from the shore. The light moved back and forth as if it were searching for us, but it never quite touched us. No doubt it *was* a land-based checkpoint.

Now we raced toward the open seas. The waves grew higher, and water started pouring over the stern onto the six of us stretched out on the floor. I was sure we would be swamped and capsize. But the captain kept going. He started to sing. We were desperately uncomfortable and frightened, but we were happy too.

At last, we could see lights and skyscrapers appearing on the horizon. We reached the spot where we were supposed to make contact with a local boat. As it turned out, the connection was never completed because our captain got lost—it had been many years since he had been in these waters. After searching fruitlessly, our captain decided to run the boat ashore on purpose. Spotting some rocks running out into the sea from a promontory, the captain moved alongside them as carefully as he could, "Go," he said. "Now." We leaped out, followed by the captain, who had opened the seacock so the boat would sink. I clung to my beloved violin and nothing else. We had made it to the shores of Hong Kong!

Wet, shivering, and ecstatic, we stood up, breathed deeply, and ripped off the Mao Zedong badges and communist slogans we had been forced to wear. One by one, we ceremoniously tossed them into the black, heaving sea.

"Our lives have been given back!" shouted the captain, who found a rock cave and suggested we get some sleep until the sun rose.

Chapter 32.

Siwu Becomes Collateral Damage

思武血灑上海

Mao followers bring to the Cultural Revolution to Shanghai

While we celebrated our good fortune in escaping Mao's clutches, my thoughts turned to my older brother Siwu and his beloved Zhuge. The rumor was that the Revolution now dominated affairs in Shanghai. Tatzepaos were attached to buildings everywhere, and vicious young adults marched and shouted in the street.

Siwu saw the revolution taking hold. He thought it best to maintain a low profile as a sincere and loyal French teacher with an obedient wife at the university. It was best not to be seen as well-dressed. He urged Zhuge to empty the closets of her high heels. They also just let their beloved dog become a stray in the streets.

Besides teaching, Siwu was very careful with whom he talked. He had no idea whom he could trust. He and Zhuge never engaged in political discussions, seldom socialized with others, and kept their opinions to themselves. Siwu figured if he remained controversy-free and followed all the authority rules, he'd be lost in the raucous crowd of hysteria.

The strategy worked for a while, but stories began to appear about my bold escape with headlines like, "Favorite son becomes a treasonous demon." Soon, these stories circulated through the Red Guard.

In May, five months after our escape, the Central Government announced the launch of yet another movement, the "Clean Class Troops." Teachers should be shaping students' minds with *only* the teachings of Mao; the initiative was designed to identify any teachers who might be doing otherwise. Once identified, these "misguided teachers" would be sent to hard labor and education camps.

The initiative was launched all over China. Within weeks, tatzepao were placed all over Shanghai Foreign College. The Revolution leaders assumed the school was a breeding ground for self-indulgent European thinking. While the teachers said nothing to each other, they were terrified they might be accused of treason since the Red Guards needed no evidence beyond making the accusation.

One day, before Siwu left for school, he and Zluge warmly embraced and kissed goodbye as usual; Zluge handed him a lunch box packed with a bit of "special treat" for being such a wonderful husband—two extra roasted eggs. Neither had any idea an angry bunch of Red Guards was waiting for Siwu at school.

As he entered the main hall, he saw two large *tatzepaos* with red crosses, and his name reversed.

Ma Sicong Betray Country. Ma Siwu Offered Planner.

He was dragged to the elevator and taken to a high floor, where Red Guards pounded the table as they investigated Siwu. Other teachers watched and shook with horror.

"Why did your brother become a traitor to our glorious revolution?" yelled one.

"We know you met your traitorous brother at the train station when he fled Beijing to Shanghai. How did you help him escape?"

Siwu explained, "My younger brother makes his own decisions." The answer infuriated the Guards. They kept asking for any useful information. Siwu had none to offer because he didn't know anything.

A tall Red Guard walked over and slapped him in the face. Siwu's head snapped back. The Guard hit him again. Blood started to drip from his lip. Two other Guards dragged him to an open window. A scuffle ensued. What happened next is not clear. But seconds later, Siwu's body sailed down 14 floors to his death. The incident was officially listed as a suicide.

According to eyewitnesses, the expressionless Red Guards looked out the window to make sure he was dead, then left.

Traveling and hiding at the time, I knew none of this.

Chapter 33.

Hong Kong to America

從香港去美國

Ma's niece in Hong Kong, soprano Nancy Zi,
helped his family get to the United States

My emotions were mixed. I was sad and humiliated. Eighteen years ago, I was in such high spirit and full of hope for the new China after the civil war. But Chairman Mao disappointed the masses, and I was forced to flee. The question was, to where? Many places had advantages and disadvantages, including Hong Kong, Europe, and Canada, among others.

I sought the advice of an experienced traveler. My niece Nancy Zi, well-connected in Hong Kong social circles, was born in the United States and raised in China. Nancy had built a career as an internationally recognized soprano who weaved ancient Eastern disciplines with modern Western techniques in her arias.

~

Somehow, the captain got Nancy's address and phone number and arranged for me to talk to her in the privacy of a small restaurant owned by his cousin in Kowloon.

"Nancy, this is uncle Sicong. I am in Hong Kong."

"Thank goodness. I've read terrible stories about the Cultural Revolution. How did you manage to escape? Where are you? I will come and get you." I was so excited I could hardly eat anything. Nancy arrived in a black limousine an hour later. She was, as I remembered—a beautiful and elegant woman the Ma family much admired. Nancy's high fashion style seemed out of place at this simple family-operated restaurant. We hugged, quickly exchanged greeting, and left. I didn't want to draw attention in a public place, still so close to the Mainland.

~

As we drove, Nancy explained that she had arranged for us to stay with her cousin, Hsu Zengchu(*se-sun-chen*), who I had known since childhood, was married to a well-respected Hong Kong physician, Doctor Kin Lin. Their house was in Kowloon, so Nancy's car could avoid the overcrowded freight boat to Hong Kong, reducing the risk of recognition.

It was apparent when we arrived that Zengchun had arranged to keep our presence in Hong Kong a private matter. The windows were covered with heavy curtains that blocked the light, and most of the servants, including the chatty gardener, a known gossip, had been given the day off.

"I have kept my chef because he is discreet and a great cook," said Zengchun. "I assumed you might be hungry after such difficult travels." Muli, Celia, and Julon nodded. Zengchun pulled back a sliding door to the dining room. A large Canton Dian Xin (dim sum) sat with shrimp, taro, chive, Teochew (*chow-chow*) dumplings, spring rolls stuffed with chicken, bamboo, and tofu, and a variety of traditional buns, soaps, and cakes. It had been a long time since any of us experienced such delicious food. We ate and drank for hours, and I explained the details of our escape.

~

Nancy looked at her watch. "Before you go to sleep, we should discuss relocation options." Muli expressed an immediate preference to stay in Hong Kong. Nancy shook her head. "The Hong Kong government would not resist the Chinese government's pressure to return you to China. These days, Hong Kong authorities always follow Chinese government demands, and the British will offer little resistance."

I suggested France since I had lived there, spoke French, and had friends, contacts, and a musical reputation. Nancy again respectfully disagreed. "France has just established diplomatic relations with China, so it might not be in their best interests to accept you. Uncle, the last thing you want is to be the subject of a political dispute."

She was right, so we discussed several other European countries, but all had some practical impediments. For example, Taiwan could probably not guarantee a haven based on my inside knowledge of Cultural Revolution atrocities and Mao's disdain for Chiang Kai-shek's Kuomintang party, which now ruled Taiwan.

~

As we talked, the conclusion became evident to Nancy, a graduate of Milliken University in Illinois. "I would suggest the United States. It is a wealthy, powerful country filled with immigrants, it has a rich love of classical music, and they are unlikely to deport you to China since political relations are strained over lack of human rights and the general distrust of Mao." I liked the idea because we had friends in the United States, and my family was fluent in English.

Nancy immediately phoned a relative working at the American consulate. In no time, the American vice-consul Martin Lee arrived at Nancy's house with forms to complete. Nancy helped complete them and handed them to Martin. "Uncle," she said, "I know you had to travel light during your escape, but where is your violin?" I was embarrassed to tell her I had used my violin as a ransom but didn't have the money to redeem it.

Nancy smiled, "I'll get your violin back under one condition. I receive complimentary tickets to your first performance at Lincoln Center in New York."

I said, "That's a deal." Then I wrote the boat owner's name and phone number on paper and handed it to Nancy.

~

Two days later, Ambassador Lee arrived with a nervous British counterpart, introduced only as K.K. They brought Celia and me into a room at the Windsor office building. Lee, who spoke fluent Mandarin, had many questions about our treatment, our escape, and the masses' attitude toward Chairman Mao and his Cultural Revolution. Lee took copious notes and recorded our statements. K.K. acted merely as an observer.

The next day, Lee and K.K. showed up at Dr. Lin's house unannounced. K.K. was holding some newspapers and paced back and forth. Lee said, "You folks have to leave Hong Kong right now! The papers and TV stations have reported your presence in Hong Kong. President Johnson told me to get you on a flight to America." For the next few hours, we remained in safety at the American Consulate.

Lee handed me part of a recent CIA report to President Lyndon Johnson. The post said, in part:

"Mao is riding the tiger with his Cultural Revolution but refuses to get off because of the tremendous loss of face and political power that would certainly end the revolution. Given that situation, we see even greater trouble ahead with, perhaps a collapse into total anarchy."

The report predicted that "before final chaos came to pass," one of two scenarios would emerge. China would return to some warlord regionalism like that which marked the 1920s. A coalition of more "moderate" military and Communist Party leaders will ease Mao aside —using him as a symbol but keeping his hand off the throttle. The agency concluded that "the second course is more likely, and that it may come to pass with the next year."

My reply was based purely on my personal experiences. "I believe Mao's teachings are more pervasive than you imagine. The Revolution will not end in a year."

Soon, it was time to go with the Secret Service nearby. Lee told us the President had ordered him to escort us to ensure no political delays or red tape. Over the next few years, I would come to realize that granting my family asylum was a political decision that offered President Johnson public relations leverage to embarrass Chairman Mao in front of the world's powers. It had little or nothing to do with my musical legacy.

~

We arrived at the airport in Washington DC at 5:00 A.M. under the assumed last name of Lee. The sky was still dark, and the ground was covered with snow. I remember thinking, *although I am no longer in China, I am confident I'll return to my homeland when the current political unrest subsides.*

We were driven to a pleasant house in the rolling hills of Virginia by a US State Department official. "You should be safe and comfortable here until we locate permanent housing."

Four months later, a press conference was held in New York City. It was attended by reporters from all over the world, except for certain pro-Communist countries, which ignored the proceedings entirely. The room was in chaos, with reporters shouting constant questions. There were so many lights and cameras that the electrical fuses failed, and the place went dark on several occasions. Eventually, the Secret Service had to restore order.

After opening remarks by the State Department, the conference was opened to questions. One reporter asked about my relationship with Chairman Mao and Premier Zhou Enlai. Another wanted to know how a person once considered a "national treasure" could fall from grace. Some of the questions were hard to answer, but I did my best for two hours.

I quickly realized I was the most public figure to have escaped China's oppressive living conditions and harsh penal system. I explained how hundreds of Central Conservatory of Music teachers were routinely forced into hard labor because they committed the crime of believing in the free rights of man and in an economy where rewards were based on honest effort rather than corrupt officials.

I explained I had been more fortunate than most because I was merely locked up and physically abused for more than 50 days but was not sentenced to death or hard labor. Instead, I was released from "study school" with slogans of guilt painted all over my body. The press clamored for more specifics. I raised my hand to stop. "There are many people still living in China who helped us escape. They remain in grave danger, so I cannot disclose specific names and places".

~

Soon, all the Chinese Communist secret service leaders were directed to investigate the details of my escape and imprison any friends and relatives that might have been involved. The order was called "002 Special Case." On January 28, 1968, the official conclusion read, "Ma Sicong betrayed the country and our benevolent leader by going over to the enemy, and is now sentenced to death."

~

The subsequent bits of information I received was also filled with untruths and exaggerations. I wanted to set the record straight, so I agreed to write about my life during the Cultural Revolution for *Life Magazine*, America's most widely-read news magazine at the time.

Subsequently, a Russian literary journal reprinted the story. Ten thousand Mao sympathizers held a massive demonstration in front of the Russian Embassy, accusing the government of using American propaganda to weaken China by undermining the Cultural Revolution. Back in Peking, angry mobs of Red Guards burned magazine copies in Tiananmen Square in the center of the city at the base of an enormous Chairman Mao monument.

Chapter 34.

Bad News in Bunches

一連串壞消息

Ma's and Muli's families become casualties of the Cultural Revolution

Life became quiet and serene for months after the press conference and magazine story.

The American Government provided pleasant temporary housing among the rolling hills of Virginia as we searched for permanent quarters. Soon, we settled down in Bethesda, Maryland, a friendly and cosmopolitan Washington DC suburb.

The house had plenty of room for Muli, me, and the children. It also contained an exquisite Japanese garden and a swimming pool. The State Department told us it was a gift of the American people with no return expectations. Soon, Muli was using her talents to blend antique and contemporary furnishings into a comfortable home. The children were getting a good education at local schools, and I had all the room I needed to do what I loved—compose and play music. While I knew China would do everything possible to smudge my reputation, the United States had a reputation for giving immigrants every chance to contribute to their new homeland. During these early days in our new land, I imagined—foolishly perhaps—that one day I would return to my roots in a peaceful, orderly, unified China.

~

Soon, my oldest sister, Sijin, called from Canada. I assumed she called to congratulate us on our escape and that we would be close enough to visit without the fear of government interference.

"Sister, so good to hear your voice." There was a long pause. "Sijin, are you there?"

"Yes, Ma." Said a weeping Sijin. "I have terrible news. Siwu is dead!"

I was stunned. "What happened?"

"I don't know all the details in the reports say Siwu accidentally fell from a 14th-floor school window."

I was angry. "I know those animals, and it was not an accident; Siwu was murdered!" We spoke a bit longer, but I was so inconsolable that I don't remember anything else Sijin said.

From time to time, Muli and I had nightmares thinking of Siwu and other relatives who might be trying to escape to Hong Kong. Nightmares night after night, for several months; we had to rely on sleeping pills to seek a moment of peace.

~

Soon, the State Department put me in contact with another friend who had recently escaped China. That was how we learned that all of Muli's family had been sentenced to seven years of hard labor in some remote area camp for helping us to escape. Muli burst into tears and asked, "Is there any news about my mother?"

"Yes," responded the man. "Before her children were arrested, they asked a neighbor to watch over her, given Huang Jing was 80 years old and lived alone in Guangdong. Several days later, the neighbor checked on Huang Jing; she found her lifeless, sitting in a chair. Neighbors say she gave up and died of a broken heart.

The man also gave me the details regarding my mother, Huang. I knew she had lived a life filled with many pangs of sadness after the assassination of my father, Yuhung's murder, my harsh and humiliating treatment by the Red Guard, and the incarceration of my brothers and sisters. From what the man told me, she became a virtual recluse at her home in Shanghai.

"When the news of your daring escape to Hong Kong became public, she was sure the Red Guards would come and take her away or find some other way to humiliate her publicly. Sure enough, on New Year's Eve, Red Guards tore the house apart, searching for clues about you. She told them she knew nothing about your escape or where you were. They didn't believe her and decided to take all her valuable belongings as a penalty for lying. When your mother protested, the Guards tossed Huang to the ground like a rag doll, laughing and sneering. Huang had never experienced such treatment, and there was no one to protect her. She spent days with bruised ribs and a heavy heart, hoping to hear from one of her nearby neighbors. No one came. They were all visiting families, celebrating the New Year.

"The sum of all these terrible vents were just too much for her to bear. She died alone in her bed, probably on New Year's Day. When some neighbors returned a day later, they found your mother under her bed covers."

~

I tried to take my mind off these terrible matters by composing.

But the bad news continued to arrive. My oldest brother Siqui and his family had become casualties of the Cultural Revolution. When I was fleeing the Red Guards, my kind and loving brother had given me money twice.

The Red Guard determined he was an assistant to a traitor, and he fell victim to a sham trial. In a matter of minutes, Siqui was found guilty of "conspiring" to help me betray my country and go over to the enemy. Siqui lost his job, and both he and his wife, Li Wei, were ordered to perform hard labor for three years.

Their 30-year old daughter, who lived nearby, underwent brutal questioning at the police station, where she died because of a heart ailment died. His second son was sentenced to 12 years of hard labor, and Siqui's youngest son, who was only a high school student, was sentenced to nine years.

I was heartbroken. I even thought of suicide to relieve the pain. But that would be a selfish act. I decided to put my sadness, pain, and yearning into my music. I remembered a nostalgic ancient Tang Dynasty poem about losing a loved one.

> To meet is hard, to part as hard to fare.
> The East Wind being faint, all flowers sear.
> Spring silkworm, dead at last, stops yielding silk;
> Wax candle, burned to ash, dries then its tear.
> O'er morning mirror, her hair changed to grieve.
> In night chant, brunt of moonlight chill she'd bear.
> From here to Fairy Mount is not so far,
> Blue Bird, be kind to visit oft my dear!

Surprisingly, I was able to turn the poem into a haunting violin solo. During the next several dark months, I did the same with several other famous Chinese poems—*Endless Lovesickness, Hard Life, Separation,* and *Farewell,* among others.

~

While I was pleased with this surprising burst of creativity, I experienced no personal comfort in the hell that I was living. But there was one small consolation—my mother was spared watching her sons and daughters murdered, humiliated, forced into hard labor camps, and fleeing for their lives.

Chapter 35.

Lincoln Center Debut

林肯中心首次亮相

紐約崇正會敦聘馬思聰教授舉行音樂會籌募福利基金

Under the Distinguished Patronage of
His Excellency Ambassador S. K. CHOW
Republic of China, Washington, D. C.
and
His Excellency Ambassador LIU CHIEH
Chinese Permanent Mission to the
United Nations, New York
Consul General of the Republic of China, K. P. YU

A BENEFIT RECITAL BY

Sitson Ma Violinist

SAMUEL SANDERS at the piano

CONCERT FOR THE BENEFIT OF THE TSUNG–TSIN MUTUAL AID ASSOCIATION

PHILHARMONIC HALL • LINCOLN CENTER
TUESDAY – JANUARY 7th 1969 – 8:30 P.M.

Ma's sold-out concert in America for the benefit of Taiwan.

To understand why I performed my concert in the United States for the Hong Kong and Taiwan-based Tsung-Tsin Mutual Aid Association requires some further understanding of China's complex post-civil war history.

~

In 1895, the Qing Dynasty ceded the Taiwan Province to Japan after winning the first Sino-Japanese war. But when the Japanese surrendered at the end of World War II, the Allies handed administrative control of Taiwan to Chiang Kai-shek's Kuomintang-led Republic of China. Local citizens quickly became resentful of what they saw as corrupt conduct by the Kuomintang authorities, including arbitrary seizure of private property, economic mismanagement, and exclusion from political participation. Civil unrest led to citizen massacres, and martial law was declared by Taiwan's governor, my father's childhood friend Chen Cheng.

During these turbulent times, the Chinese Civil War broke out on the mainland between Chiang Kai-skek's Republic of China forces and Mao's Communist Party of China. In 1949, Chiang was defeated; he moved to Taiwan, declared Taipei the temporary capital, took military control of the government, and nationalized private industry.

Chairman Mao, preoccupied with consolidating his political power, establishing various movements, and creating the Cultural Revolution, thought Taiwan was too insignificant to waste military and other resources to recapture.

Chiang maintained a well-equipped military in case Mao and the mainlanders tried to invade Taiwan. He quickly realized that maintaining high-level diplomatic relations in Washington and New York required outside funding from successful Chinese loyalists, who had long since fled the mainland. One of the ways funds were raised was by holding cultural events in high-visibility locations. These events were usually arranged by the Tsung-Tsin Mutual Aid Association, a Hong Kong-based nonprofit organization. At the same time, the Taiwanese ambassadors managed the wire transfer of the gross receipts through a network of international banks. Mao and his officials protested the activities, but the U.S. government just turned a blind eye.

~

About seven months after my arrival, I was asked to perform a solo concert at the world-famous Philharmonic Hall in Lincoln Center for the cause. I was happy to oblige, given my family's poor treatment at the hands of Mao supporters and the fact that many of my friends starved to death during China's Great Famine.

I developed the Lincoln Center program in two parts. For lack of a better term, the first half showcased Western classical masterpieces, including Veracini's *Konzert - Sonate e Moll*, Bach's *Chaconne*, Schubert's *Duo A Major Op. 162*. The second half of the program showcased my compositions, including *Mountain Song, Dragon Lantern Song, Pastoral, 1st. Rondo*, and *Mongolian Suite*. During rehearsals, I was impressed by the quality and purity of the sound in such a large hall.

The Tsung-Tsin Association publicized the event to the wealthy expatriate membership and ran press releases and news stories in Chinese-American papers. The sold-out benefit raised hundreds of thousands of dollars for Taiwan. I took nothing—other than two complimentary tickets for my niece, Nancy Li, and her husband, who traveled from Hong Kong for the event.

"I'm very proud of you, Ma, " said a beaming Nancy at the cocktail party later that evening.

"Without your help, my music and I would not be here," I replied.

The critics were kind, which helped to establish my reputation in the United States. One even commented that "Ma's violin compositions illustrate what can be achieved by the marriage of Eastern and Western musical traditions, which we understand Mao Zedong wishes to suppress for all time."

~

Not long after the concert, I received a note from friends that my sister-in-law, Zluge, 43, had returned to France and died of a broken heart. The letter said she never got over the loss of her husband, my kind, gentle brother Siwu.

Chapter 36.

My Friend, The Spy

我的朋友，间谍

William Clothier, 86, Spy and Tennis Star

By The Associated Press

Nov. 3, 2002

William J. Clothier II, a former tennis star, international spy and grandson of the co-founder of the Strawbridge & Clothier department store chain in the Philadelphia area, died here on Oct. 19. He was 86.

While Mr. Clothier won national tennis titles, he was also secretly a special agent for the F.B.I. and later worked for the C.I.A.

Mr. Clothier, whose father, William J. Clothier, was a national singles champion, toured on the grass-court tennis circuit from 1934 to 1938. Together, the two won a national father-son title twice.

In his government work, Mr. Clothier was an F.B.I. special agent in Peru, Cuba and Chile in World War II. He used his 1938 bachelor's degree in anthropology from Harvard as a cover. From 1952 to 1979, Mr. Clothier was a C.I.A. officer, gathering intelligence and aiding defectors.

Something Ma never realized about his close friend.

In the spring of 1969, while we were living in Bethesda, Celia decided she might want to study at the University of Pennsylvania, so she drove up for a tour. One of her guides was a handsome doctoral candidate in physical chemistry named Cheng Ken Chi. Three months later, Celia announced she and Ken had fallen in love and planned to marry and live in Pennsylvania until he finished school. I laughed; she had the same determined tone as her mother.

I got to meet the young man before he formally proposed to her in our Japanese garden that same June! He was bright and respectful and appeared to come from a loving family.

~

Then Celia's younger brother, Julon, decided he wanted to attend Temple University in Philadelphia.

The fates had spoken. I had zero interest or aptitude in homeowner chores like gardening and repairs; my passion was composing music. Muli agreed. So we moved to Philadelphia to be close to our family.

~

We found a lovely apartment on the 14th floor of an apartment building that overlooked scenic Fairmount Park.

Muli again decorated our home to make it pleasing and comfortable to minds and eyes. I can still remember almost every last detail. The windowsills were always full of seasonal flowers and green plants, and the top of our French chiffonier near the window was dotted with annual indoor plants. The lighted China cabinet was filled with personal artifacts from our travels to Europe and Asia; our baby grand piano had an unusual lamp, which created a romantic atmosphere at night. The walls were covered with Chinese paintings and calligraphies.

Soon Celia was pregnant with our first granddaughter, Ida. To care for Ida, Ken and Celia moved in with us. Muli often bathed Ida as an infant. The inexperienced Celia was afraid to put Ida into the water for fear of drowning. Muli and I enjoyed being grandparents, but Ken and Celia moved to Indiana when Ken got a postdoctoral job at Purdue University before we knew it. We missed them so

Much that Muli and I drove thousands of miles to see them. We were also able to meet some of our long-lost friends in Chicago. They became our tour guides to show us everyday democracy at work in America.

We visited several American Civil War sites. I was surprised to find many unfortunate similarities to the Chinese history of revolutions. In my society, people revolted for political control, power, and greed. It was not uncommon for princes in the same family to kill each other to maintain or gain power. To Muli and me, the American Civil War was different. It was a human-rights revolt that pitted brothers against brothers over the use of people as slaves. In China, there are no slaves, just hundreds of millions of poor laborers made to feel less than human. I wondered, was there a difference?

~

We never imagined that Ken and Celia would move even further away, but Ken was offered an excellent job as Researcher II at the University of California in Los Angeles. Muli and I made the best of it. We took several cross-country flights and drove to many southern California cultural and tourist attractions by car, amazed at the extensive superhighway system. Luckily, after two short years in Los Angeles, Ken and Celia moved back to Philadelphia, where Ken assumed a research associate job at the University of Pennsylvania.

~

Ken and Celia lived only two blocks away from us. Celia would bring Ida to spend the whole day with Muli and me; Ida was our playful little jewel. Muli, who had become quite the skilled cook, would share recipes in the kitchen for hours.

I loved to play box with Ida, who was well-coordinated and quite competitive for her age. I quickly learned she did not like to lose. She invented imaginary "smart" and "foolish" boxing pills. Before we began every fight, Ida would take a smart pill and then trick me into taking a foolish pill. She was convinced the smart pill made her faster and more challenging to hit. The foolish pill made me slower, and Ida would win. As I lay on the imaginary canvas, she would jump up and down with a victory cheer. About one in a hundred times, Ida would "mistakenly" take the foolish pill and lose. She wanted to make sure I remained interested in future matches.

~

Celia got pregnant for a second time, so we decided we needed a larger home in Philadelphia. The State Department introduced us to businessman Bill Clothier II and his family, who knew the area well. Bill Clothier was part of an aristocratic Pennsylvania family. His grandfather was the co-founder of the iconic Strawbridge & Clothier department stores. His father was an American national tennis champion, and Bill Clothier carried on the family tradition by winning a national doubles championship as a father-son team.

We often socialized with Bill and his wife, Irene, and soon they became close friends. We had much in common; they loved Muli's Chinese cooking, and Bill and I shared a love of fine wines, particularly French.

Irene was born in Germany and looked like the movie star Lauren Bacall. They had twins, Morris and Steffanie, born prematurely and weighed less than six pounds together. They marveled at how lucky we were to have such a healthy granddaughter. Bill and Irene were loving parents, and they watched their children closely. In time, their kids became healthy teenagers.

~

On sunny weekends, the two families would drive toward the Poconos and visit a well-known flower farm with a gorgeous mountain top that always seemed to be decorated with seasonal flowers. It was a spectacular sight, as was a trail leading to the top.

Muli, Irene, and the kids would race to the top and return with all kinds of flowers and plants. Sometimes we'd go for a hike at nearby Green Valley in Fairmount Park. Life seemed to be full.

Weekends also had food rituals. We would all go for dinner at my favorite Chinese restaurant, the Riverside, in Philadelphia's Chinatown. The place was bustling and always had long waiting lines. The restaurant owner was a fan of classical music, which played over the loudspeakers. As he handed us the menus one evening, my composition *Nostalgia* began to play. I pointed to the speaker, then to myself. The man ran into the kitchen and returned with one of my albums. He was ecstatic. I autographed the cover.

From that moment on, we always got the best table and were never made to wait. The owner would ask the chef to make off-menu dishes with unique new ingredients or fresh supplies. The foods were a feast for the eyes, nose, and mouth. The aromas would fill the restaurant. Inevitably, the commotion surrounding us made the other guests jealous. They didn't get that same level of attentive service, and the dishes we ate weren't on the menu. One evening, a patron complained. "Why is this man treated so special?"

The restaurant owner replied proudly, "Because he is special. This is Ma Sicong."

~

The fun-loving Irene had a low, sexy voice that sounded like Marlene Dietrich. By contrast, Bill was generally quiet and reserved until we shared a bottle of wine or two in my study. Usually, we talked about simple matters, but this one evening in 1971, he seemed most curious about my past relationships with Zhou Enlai and Chairman Mao. He wondered how my father and I could be close friends of a mortal enemy—Chiang Kai-shek—yet coexist with the current Communist regime. I didn't realize Bill knew anything about my father. I became curious.

"Why such interest in Chinese matters?" I asked.

He laughed, "Because you're my good friend, of course." I wasn't sure I believed him, but I said nothing. Soon Celia delivered granddaughter Nina. Celia and Muli made sure they saw the children almost every day. One night, when Ida reached school age, I mentioned to Bill that we lived in a neighborhood with an abysmal public-school reputation.

He replied, "You're right, but those matters can be fixed." That semester, with letters of recommendation from Bill and other people I didn't know, Celia entered a well-regarded and expensive private school called Friends School. When I asked the principal if I could pay the tuition bill in installments, she smiled and said, "It's all taken care of."

~

Muli and I decided to thank the Clothiers by buying dinner at one of Philadelphia's oldest restaurants, Snockey's Oyster and Crab House on South Street. Bill was surprised and pleased.

"We Chinese do like oysters and clams," I laughed.

The conversation turned to children. "Celia and Julon are such well-mannered, respectful young adults," said Irene.

"What about Bixue," asked Bill.

"How do you know about Bixue?"

"Ma, it's my job to know."

"Who is Bixue?" asked Irene.

"She *was* our oldest daughter," I replied.

"I don't understand."

"Bixue became an active member of the Communist Party while in college. She tried to have me reported and embarrassed about my views. We haven't spoken in more than 20 years."

Irene was now curious. "And Julon, Why is he always with you. What did he do?"

"Julon's situation is different," I said. "Muli and I love Julon unconditionally. But, he has Autism, which has reduced his ability to socialize. As a result, Muli and I have taken on the responsibility of watching and protecting him. He is a loving son who we know will take excellent care of us in our old age."

~

Bill Clothier died in 2002, 15 years after Ma. His obituary, "Tennis Star and Spy," appears at the front of this chapter. Chances are, had Ma still been alive; he might have been surprised but not shocked.

Chapter 37.

Taiwan,

Home Away from Home

台湾，我的家外之家

Ma visits family friend, President Chiang Kai-shek in Taipei.

In March 1970, Muli and I received an invitation to celebrate Taiwan's annual music festival, which brought thousands of Taiwanese to Taipei each year.

As I explained to reporters at the airport, "Taiwan's audiences are like a hometown audience. I look forward to performing for them.

"Taiwan is a familiar place for me. I performed here in 1929 and 1946. I made many friends in music circles. I would love to see how they are doing."

Our first stop was the offices of the Republic of China, President Chiang Kai-Shek. Initially, we spoke of old times—both good and bad. "Ma, your father was my good old friend. He gave me much sound advice about the creation of a new Republic." He paused. "I have two sadnesses at this stage of my life—that the mystery of your father's murder was never solved, and my disappointment with the abrupt turnaround of your new President Nixon."

As Chiang explained, Nixon, a private citizen, made trips to Taiwan in 1964 and '67 as Chiang Kai-shek's houseguest. Chiang asked for America's support in joining the United Nations as a sovereign county. But once in office, Nixon declared America would follow the One-China Principle, which assumed Taiwan was part of China and would eventually be unified by peaceful or non-peaceful means.

I did not wish to engage in a political discussion. "Sir," I said, "I am a musician."

He nodded. "And a damn fine one. Please think of Taiwan as your home, and you should come home as often as possible."

~

For the next two weeks, Muli and I toured the country and performed before tens of thousands of enthusiastic fans in Taiwan's four largest cities (Taipei, Kaohsiung, Taichung, and Tainan).

At the end of the tour, we held a press conference before returning to the United States. I found the questions stimulating and worthy of reprinting. I hope the reader will accept my temporary indulgence.

A reporter from Taiwan's leading newspaper, *China Times*, asked, "It is common knowledge that you and Chairman Mao had sharp differences in musical philosophy. So what road do you feel China's music should walk?"

"I believe music should not travel one road. No one, including Mao, can force that upon a people's culture. I feel China's music must deliver innovative compositions that accommodate our rich traditions while at the same time celebrating other countries' musical achievements. In this way, new Chinese-inspired classics can stand on firm foundations that endure. I recognize this blended state of music cannot be embraced in a short period, but we must diligently walk in this direction. Our job as artists is for listeners to recognize this is the new Chinese music quickly."

Another reporter asked, "What role do folklore and symbolism play in your music?"

"Before composing, a composer should immerse himself in civil society to understand a country's folklore and symbolism and how it has entered our music. At the same time, the artist needs to avoid the ease of plagiarism, so he develops an original musical voice that is his alone.

"I also believe the music symbols a composer employs must express his real thoughts and passion and should not be filled with pretense or effect. The feelings the artist has the desire to express must come from a sincere heart."

During the trip, I also received the honorary title of Philosopher Extraordinaire, the nation's highest cultural award, from the highly respected China Academy

~

When Muli and I left Taiwan, we continued our tour in Southeast Asia, performing in Cambodia, Laos, the Philippines, and Singapore, where we were made welcome by the local people and their leaders.

I was most impressed by King Rama IX in Bangkok, Thailand. He had read much about me and was most interested in my music. He asked if I might perform a private concert at a suitable hall inside the king's mansion. I was delighted at the request. I decided to play *Nostalgia,* which I realized had become my signature composition, the foundation of my musical legacy. The king and his staff appeared mesmerized. He asked if I had time to continue. I looked at my watch and realized we needed to get to the airport because of the scheduled stops. "Respectfully, I have to decline because of prior commitments."

The king was gracious, "I understand."

~

Days later, on the plane back to America, Muli asked what seemed an odd question. "If Mao and Zhou asked you to play for them, would you return?"

My response: "Confucius says the man who stands on the hill with mouth open will wait a long time for roast duck to drop in."

Muli never asked that question again.

Chapter 38.

Sunset Glow

晚霞

Turning a mystical short story into a four-act ballet

Returning home from Taiwan, I felt refreshed and in need of a new musical challenge.

On the plane back to America, I began to read *Strange Stories from the Lodge of Leisure* by Pu Songling, a 300-year-old collection of classic Chinese short stories that implicitly criticized the Qing Dynasty's social problems while blending them with mystical symbolism.

I became captivated by the story *Sunset Glow*. All Chinese know that dance became almost extinct because of Qing suppression. What surprised me was that Pu's manner of protest incorporated the beauty of dancing into *Sunset Glow*. He made the dancers, their costumes, and movements—both in this world and the story's undersea palace—precise and vivid. I saw no need for me to make any improvements; the pages were filled with righteous indignation. What I had to do was set the epic story to music.

The Story of Sunset Glow
By Pu Songling
During the annual dragon-boat festival, the dragon-boat race scene was most lively, bustling with noise. Youngsters stood at bow and stern, hanging high on ropes, performing dangerous acts to please the masses.

One of the youngsters, the graceful and vigorous A-Duan, fell into the water while performing, drowned, and was directed to enter the undersea dragon palace, which was bustling with songs and dances. Soon, A-Duan mastered all dances with the help of a teacher named Jie Lao.

One day, the undersea dragon king watched his dancing troupes—Yaksha, Nightingale, Swallow, Willow, and Golden Glow—perform. It became evident that Sunset Glow was the most outstanding and elegant dancer. A-Duan, watching nearby, was enthralled by her.

A-Duan followed with a fast dance and vivid posture that won the king's praise, rewarded him with a silk robe and pearl crown. When all started to depart, Sunset Glow purposefully left her hairpins, and A-Duan, swimming nearby, picked them up. From that day on, A-Duan dreamed about Sunset Glow day and night and languished by the thoughts. It was love at first sight for Sunset Glow also, but both were too shy and embarrassed to communicate their mutual longings directly.

Fortunately, a mutual friend, butterfly boy Joe Lao, brought them together at a beautiful lotus flower pond. There, the couple exchanged their innermost feelings of love and pledged to marry without parental permission. The flower fairies danced to celebrate two lovers becoming a couple.

The dragon king brought his dancing troupes to his Wu River Palace to celebrate his birthday one day. But Sunset Glow was left behind to teach dancing elsewhere in the kingdom. Months passed, and she could not return home. A-Duan and Sunset Glow missed each other deeply. Deep depression set into Sunset Glow's heart, which eventually caused her death.

When A-Duan got the shocking news, he felt great desperation and committed suicide. Their love moved the great jade emperor. He not only brought A-Duan back to life together with his mother but also his lover Sunset Glow. They lived happily together ever after.

Like a plant seed, *Sunset Glow* began to grow as soon as it fell to the soil that was me. My goal was to a beautiful music composition that would live for centuries. I decided I would weigh every syllable as I worked and devote my remaining years to its perfection.

As it came to be, the ballet drama grew to four acts with eleven scenes and 42 original compositions. It took me almost a decade to complete and went through eight extensive revisions.

I think the epic nature of *Sunset Glow* is most like Richard Wagner's operatic masterpiece, *The Ring*, which was created in four parts and took two decades to produce.

~

When complete, *Sunset Glow* was an imposing drama that contained oriental artistic charm blended with occidental music techniques. I also decided to rename it *A Romance in The Dragon Palace*. It was initially performed in Taiwan at the cost of US $250,000US ($1 million in today's dollars).

The highly-publicized world premiere embarrassed China's leader, Deng Xiaoping (*deng-show-ping*), who had risen to power after the deaths of Mao Zedong and Zhou Enlai. He considered Taiwan merely a rebellious colony that belonged to China. While Deng supported socialist ideology with a selected free-market enterprise—otherwise known as Socialism with Chinese Characteristics—he remained fully committed to absolute Communist single-party rule.

Secondly, Deng found my motivations disrespectful. He openly wondered how a native, who had once served as his country's musical ambassador, could reject his homeland by premiering an essential cultural work outside the mainland.

~

A Romance in the Dragon Palace was enjoyed by the audiences and received high praise from the press. I was also pleased to be introduced as "*our* gifted and morally courageous person who fought Chinese Party oppression." Slowly but surely, Taiwan felt like home.

Chapter 39.

Discovering Mountain Music

發現高山族音樂

Ma was fascinated by the sounds of the A-Mei's tribal music.

While the United States was not my homeland, Muli and I were always made to feel welcome.

In April 1972, I performed a sold-out concert at the Los Angeles Philharmonic to raise the profile of Taiwan as a sovereign nation. After the show, Muli and I were given the city's key, and the day was proclaimed Ma Sicong Day. Local Chinese community leaders also gave Muli and me a gold plaque to show their appreciation for our fund-raising activities.

~

Nevertheless, after Mao and Zhou died eight months apart in 1976, I thought seriously about returning to China. But Muli was strongly resistant. "The struggle for political power continues, and the outspoken pro-Cultural Revolutionary politicians who want your head remain as they were. Most of all, our family lives here." I knew in my heart that Muli was right.

To connect to my Chinese roots, I visited and performed in nearby Taiwan seven times during those 20 years. There, I rekindled old friendships I had thought lost when we all fled China, and I made new international friends who loved my music and had no interest in talking politics and power. These visits and friendships brought me to think about how I would like to be remembered and why I seemed to need to push new musical boundaries.

~

On our first return trip after the worldwide debut of *A Romance in the Dragon Palace,* I visited the local A-Me and Gaoshan tribes living in the mountains. These people were considered the initial inhabitants of this previously uninhabited place. They were acknowledged as the Aborigines of Taiwan, similar to the Aborigines of the Australian outback.

The A-Mei and Gaoshan did not have a written language, so music, especially singing, became an essential means of communication and education for the Aborigines, whose culture is considered historically valuable in Taiwan. The first time we attended an A-Mei and Gaoshan performances, I was moved by their expressive folk songs and colorful, passionate dances. We spent almost a month studying these people and their cultures.

~

When I returned to the United States, I composed the *A-Meii Suite for Violin* and the *Gaoshan Suite* based on their folk music.

The *A-Meii Suite for Violin* was composed of five tunes—*Spring, Loneliness, Love Song, Moon, and Mountain Dance,* each created with a distinctly different musical imagery:

Spring used several short melodies full of joy and youth.

Loneliness used low violin chords that alternate between excitement and extreme calmness

Love Song was a playful tune that praised beauty.

Moon was a soft melody with high octaves that represented the moonlight shining on rippling lake water.

Mountain Dance used a forceful, wild, warm arpeggio rhythm to imitate the cuckoo bird's cry.

By contrast, the *Gaoshan Suite* included six tunes designed like individual paintings to describe the Gaoshans daily activities, such as drinking, battle dancing, calling dead spirits, and completing the annual harvest.

~

Later, during our 1975 visit, my friend Chiang Kai-shek died of kidney failure, and his son, friend Chiang Ching-kuo, who served as Premier, became President-in-waiting of the Republic of China. Chiang held my music in the same high regard as his father, so I was honored when he asked me to compose the orchestral music accompanying the Taiwanese national anthem. Soon, Chiang invited me to build a music Conservatory in Taiwan that would be superior to the Mainland's rundown Academy of Music. He also offered to build Muli and me a house of our choice. While I was honored, I had to decline because such a project would take too much time away from composing and performing.

Given the highs and lows I experienced on this particular trip, I was filled with desire and inspiration. In a matter of three years, I composed six major works:

Rondo for Violin No. 3
Rondo for Violin No. 4

Concerto for Double Violin
Duets for Violins
Piano Concerto in A Major
Violin Sonata No.3

While I was pleased with all the pieces, the *Concerto for Double Violins* in three movements turned out to be particularly noteworthy; it contained a heartfelt lyrical melody designed to express my love for family, especially my grandchildren. Some critics compared this piece to *Nostalgia*. I found that very rewarding since *Nostalgia* had long since become a work I knew would endure throughout the ages.

I also completed a collection of vocal solos based on famous Tang Dynasty poems, namely, *After Glow, Just an Empty Talk, A Song for Chinese Zither, Three-holed Pipe Music, Horse-galloping River, Serenity,* and *Autumn Twilight in The Mountains.*

While these musical adaptations may not have been my most significant musical works, they did offer me an outlet to provide my sadness and regrets for abandoning the citizens of my homeland, leaving them stranded to incur so many atrocities.

Like in so much of my life, there were unintended consequences related to my frequent Taiwan visits. Mao and Zhou became angry and embarrassed. Initially, I thought I would be forgotten once they died, but China's old guard did all they could to have me returned to China and brought to justice. Thanks to the State Department and whoever worked quietly behind the scenes, China failed.

~

During this phase of my roller-coaster life, I received some unexpected news from my younger sister, Siju, who was now quite an accomplished classical artist.

After exchanging pleasantries, she told me, "I've been waiting for the right moment." Out came the good news. "Remember the *Cello Concerto for A Major*?" I thought to myself, how could I forget—it was the last work I composed before the Cultural Revolution, and to the best of my knowledge, the first cello composition ever written by a Chinese composer.

"Yes," I replied.

"Father, I never told you because I wasn't sure I would ever see it again. Just before the Red Guards pillaged our house, I hid the manuscript inside the fireplace. Friends have been able to retrieve it. I will mail it to you."

Chapter 40.

Zhou's Regret

周的遺憾

Zhou and Henry share a meal, music, and private moments.

This chapter about my life has nothing and everything to do with Henry Kissinger's secret trip to China in 1971, as a precursor to President Richard Nixon's arrival months later to meet Mao Zedong.

Our friendship and my European education gave me, a musician, a unique understanding of the Mao-Zhou thought process. The two Chinese leaders shared the same world view: China would one day become the world's dominant economic and military power.

President Nixon understood that fact while his political competitors laughed at the absurdity. As Nixon wrote in private papers later, "China is not yet a military power; it is an isolated military force. But 25 years from now, they will be a decisive world factor. For us not to seek safe ways to end their total isolation would leave things in a hazardous condition for generations of Americans to come."

During 20 hours of meetings between Zhou and Kissinger, they discussed many issues, including Japanese defense policy, the future of Taiwan, the ongoing South Asian conflict over Bangladesh, the Vietnam War, details of Nixon's trip, and Chinese access to foreign markets and investment capital. Interestingly, the official notes and memos from the meeting were completed using Chinese-only translators for entirely different reasons: Kissinger feared leaks outside the White House, and Mao and Zhou wanted to always be in a position to save face at all costs. That is the Chinese way—the words "I'm sorry" do not exist in Chinese single-party politics.

While there was a level of openness between the men, it was measured. One of the significant issues that had a direct impact on my life and music was Taiwan. As far as Zhou was concerned, the island was part of China. Zhou insisted that the normalization of relations meant that the United States would remove its troops from Taiwan.

I had heard through numerous sources that Zhou was quite annoyed that I traveled freely to and from Taiwan, had scheduled a concert tour that would begin in Taipai, and had even written some new compositions that celebrated Taiwanese culture. But at that point in the evening, my name was not mentioned.

That evening over dinner, Kissinger and Zhou shared traditional Chinese food and drink. After dinner, an intimate violin concert was given in honor of Kissinger's arrival.

Soon, the violinist began to play *Nostalgia*. Kissinger, a lover of classical music, was mesmerized by the composition.

"That is a haunting but unfamiliar melody," said Kissinger.

Zhou agreed. "It is called *Nostalgia* and is probably the most famous violin composition ever created in China. The composition depicts the desperation of our oppressed nation before the Cultural

Revolution and contains classical Chinese and European influences. Ma is "*Our* National Treasure."

"Who is Ma?" asked Kissinger.

According to my sources—which I would never reveal—Zhou replied, "It was all a terrible mistake. I am deeply sorrowed about the pain, suffering, and humiliation the Cultural Revolution inflicted on my friend and his family. As I have stated to U.S. officials in Hong Kong, Ma is free to come home. There will be no further reprisals, although his preference to perform in Taiwan is inexplicable."

The savvy, diplomatic Kissinger chose not to have an opinion on Zhou's "one mistake, " despite awareness of the State Department and the CIA's role in my relocation to the United States and the subsequent publication of my *Life* magazine story. He knew further discussion of such a Mao-sensitive matter would not benefit America's normalization discussions.

He also knew my *Life* magazine escape story was Mao's worst public relations embarrassment. I was a highly-paid Chinese official who composed music with decadent bourgeois influences out of step with Mao's teachings, and I lived to tell the world about it.

~

When Kissinger returned, he briefed Nixon on what went unsaid. He knew the Chinese Communists took great care never to be embarrassed publically. Kissinger knew America's military support for Taiwan was one such embarrassment. But after dinner with Zhou, he realized my high-profile musical performances in Taiwan—despite my status as a Chinese citizen in exile—was another major embarrassment.

During the remainder of his term in office, Nixon struggled with the Taiwan military issue with many American presidents. But the "Ma" solution was different. I would be "unofficially" looked after by the CIA indefinitely. That's when I learned that my friendship with operative Bill Clothier was not an accident.

~

Shortly after the Zhou meeting, Bill and Irene Clothier were having drinks with Muli and me. I noticed Bill sitting at the desk near *my* phone. He had never done that before.

He looked at me and said, "There's a little crisis at the office that needs tending to, so I gave them your number. I hope you don't mind."

I said, "No problem."

The phone rang. Bill picked it up. "Just hang on a minute." He looked at me and said, "I need to take this call in your study." The conversation was muffled. The only thing I heard was, "I don't think there is any cause for concern. There's no chance he would return. We've given him everything he needs here, including safe passage to and from Taiwan, where he likes to perform for his buddy, Shek."

A few days later, a contact at the Taiwan Embassy—obviously a mainland mole—told me the Chinese Communist Party had sent out feelers that I would be welcome if I wished to come home. I knew it was a lie. I told Clothier about the call. I never again received such a contact.

Chapter 41.

Reconciliation

和解平反

*China's post-Cultural Revolution leader, mighty-mite Deng Xiaoping,
declares himself the people's savior.*

China's mysterious politics have always left outsiders confused. So it was in the aftermath of Mao's death in 1976.

As I read about the turmoil from afar, it seemed little had changed.

Mao's fourth wife, Jing Qing, did everything possible to maintain power during the final stages of the Cultural Revolution, with the help of The Gang of Four—Mao's vicious, politically powerful sidekicks. They imprisoned more than 250 long-time Communist Party Leaders she deemed potentially disloyal. One of them, the French-educated Deng Xiaoping, was a member of the powerful Politburo. He was known for his organizational skills and believed in individual self-interest, which was at odds with Mao's strict egalitarian policies.

Deng's plight even had analogies to my situation—once a respected member of society; he had been stripped of his posts and exiled to the rural province of Jingxi to undergo "re-education" for an unspecified length of time.

~

Shortly after Deng's exile, Jing was ousted, and the Gang of Four fell out of favor and were imprisoned or put to death for a series of treasonous crimes. When Zhou started to fail from cancer, Deng returned to political favor through a series of unspoken alliances and secret promises and was effectively put in charge of the government, the party, and the military. Soon he began to restore previously purged government officials to shore up his power base. Ordinary citizens never learned precisely how Deng went from an ostracized official to the absolute leader of the Republic of China in such a short time. But nobody was about to challenge him. The little man with the big ego was the new Mao!

Under Deng's leadership, more than 250,000 persons who had been formally investigated were cleared of charges, as well as millions who were not formally charged. Many complicated cases were also cleared by simply dismissing those wrongly accused. Even Liu Shaoqi, former PRC President, who died under harsh treatment and torture during the Cultural Revolution, was posthumously rehabilitated in 1980.

~

Deng's rallying cry became the Four Modernizations, articulated initially by Zhou Enlai—the development of industry, agriculture, defense, and science and technology. During his 13-year reign, the seeds of modern industrial China were sown.

First, he dismantled Mao's system of communes. He replaced them with a system of household responsibility whereby citizens were accountable to the state for what it agreed to produce and free to keep surpluses for private use. He also initiated experiments with capitalist methods of production, allowing private entrepreneurship to flourish. Deng explained, "It does not matter if a cat is black or white so long as it catches the mouse." As I read about these changes, it was apparent that China had awoken economically.

Deng's political reforms were controversial at the time. He wanted to develop Communist succession leadership according to legal guidelines rather than personality struggles and govern the social and political order by law, not man. [5]

~

As Deng took absolute control in the early '80s, my younger brother Si-Hon, now living in the United States, received an invitation from the Chinese government to perform several violin recitals in the major cities. Si-Hon told me it was a tearful reunion when he arrived at the Beijing airport. Siqui and many old friends also wanted to know how I was in America.

When the tour was over, Si-Hon told me he returned to the U.S. through Hong Kong, where he was surrounded by reporters who wanted to know what China's current attitude was toward me. Was

---

[5] Deng's success in political modernization is still in question. Like Mao before him, he felt the need to aggrandize his legacy. Large monuments and posters labeling Deng the "Father of the Modern Chinese Industrial Miracle" can still be found in today's China. Deng's legacy also included the Tiananmen Square massacre in 1989, where he ordered thousands of pro-democracy protesters killed and arrested because of their demands for civil equality.

my music still banned? Did I plan to return? Did his trip make plans for my return?

A Hong Kong newspaper published the following report. "Today, Ma Si-Hon confirmed that Ma Sicong's sudden escape from China during the Cultural Revolution had been solved. China's authorities told Si-Hon his brother was welcome to visit China at his convenience. Si-Hon implied his brother would be interested in such an invitation, but 'the weather is too hot right now. Maybe he visits when the weather turns cooler later in the year.' Our sources confirmed S-Hon's statement; Ma Sicong's return to China is coming soon, probably for China's National Holiday."

~

Soon, I received an oral invitation from an old friend, Li Ling, vice president of China's Music Association, China's Minister of Culture, and China's Ambassador. He said, "I have been authorized to extend an invitation to visit the 'new China.'" I was intrigued but skeptical; I sat at my study table by the window, picked up a pen, and then hesitated. I knew my response had to be carefully written because Ling was sure to show my response to his superiors.

> Brother Ling,
>   We haven't written to each other for a long time. I am glad to receive your invitation. Thank you for your interest in inviting me to visit China. My brother, Ma Si-Hon, has also mentioned welcoming me to visit China. I want to thank you and the Ambassador for such goodwill. When I assess that it is valuable and suitable for the people, it will be time to fulfill it. Good luck for now.

Muli read the letter. She knew I was uncertain. "I think that is a proper response," she said. "We have not received an official letter, just a personal invitation with no offer to pay our travel expenses, which will be more than $10,000.

Soon, a letter arrived from my *former* daughter Bixu with a Hong Kong postmark. I had no interest in reading, much less responding. The scars of her betrayal were still open. Muli decided to respond clearly but firmly.

> Bixue,
>
> Your daddy still has fears about the mainland. Every night for more than six months after we arrived in America, Daddy had the same nightmare—he was recaptured by the Red Guard and forced to return. He relived the violence of the Cultural Revolution. He saw bloodstains on his bed and clothing; his head scars were still open and fresh.
>
> Bixue, your father, and I believe there are still enemies waiting in the Communist Party; the Chinese have long memories. We have no interest in again fleeing from death with nothing but the clothes on our back.

~

Months went by, and there was still no official invitation from China's central authorities. I was unaware at the time, but voices in the Chinese government were preoccupied with my four treasonous actions: my escape to the capitalist U.S., my blasphemous New York press conference, my propaganda-ridden magazine article denouncing the Cultural Revolution, and my friendly ties and musical performances in Kuomintang-led Taiwan, which the Chinese have always maintained is a territory of the mainland.

Initially, one of the lone dissenters was Deng. His European education suggested that artfully blending Chinese musical traditions with the East was a rare achievement and celebrated in China. I have no way of proving it, but I believe he must have learned of the many positive critical reviews and my compositions earned around the world. And never once in those performances did I denigrate my homeland.

Finally, with Deng Xiaoping's approval, the voices of the opposition were silenced. The official contact came on November 10, 1984. The president of the Central Conservatory of Music, Wu Zuqiang, who had flown to America to attend a U.S.-China Music Education conference, made an official visit to our home in Philadelphia. Wu said Chairman Deng and all of China would welcome my visit "at my convenience."

I said, "How do I know my family will be safe? Remember my standing."

Wu smiled. "Leader Deng is sorry for your harsh treatment. You and your family were collateral damage in Mao's wave of unbridled enthusiasm. Before he died, even your friend Zhou expressed his greatest sorrow was what your country did to you. When you return, the Leader would very much like you to perform *Sunset Glow*. We understand it was well-received in our Taiwanese territory."

~

On December 10, the Central Conservatory of Music announced in a 6,000-word report that it recommended my complete reconciliation.

On January 24, 1985, the Minister of Culture approved that recommendation. The ban on my music was lifted, and my reputation as a national music treasure was restored in press stories. To my complete surprise, the government also repaid all my past salaries, dating back to my days at the Conservatory, and returned private properties seized during the Cultural Revolution.

On March 1, 1985, the *Beijing Evening News* announced the ban on my music had been lifted, and China National Radio would begin broadcasting the following day. For the first time in almost 20 years, my friends told me *Nostalgia* played loudly across China. About a month later, on March 31, the Shanghai Symphony Orchestra performed my signature works, *The Song of Mountain Forests* and *Nostalgia*, live for the first time since lifting the ban.

On April 2, a long-awaited official letter arrived at my Philadelphia home.

Mr. Ma Sicong,

The China Musicians Association wishes to inform you that 18 years of wrongful accusations have been redressed and your reputation fully restored. Musicians inside and outside China are ecstatic for you.

Despite the lack of a homeland during these years, you made many contributions to the music world, performing, composing, and exploring new musical directions.

During these same 18 years, music and art also made significant advancements in your motherland. Many young musicians, using your teachings as a model, have been honored at famous international competitions.

We welcome you and your family to come back for a joyful meeting and personal chatting. We also hope to see your beautiful violin technique and listen to your new works.

~

My response was cautiously congratulatory.

To All Comrades,

Thank you for your care and greeting. As you know, many people, including myself, suffered persecution and tried to escape. Some, like my older brother Siwu, were not so successful. Despite these unpleasant memories, I still congratulate the country's modernization.

Time passes so quickly. I am now an old man in my 70s. I hope I am given the time and strength to finish a few new works as my small contribution to the development of Chinese music. Regarding my return, we do want to visit relatives, old friends and touch the ground of our beloved motherland. It has been too long. I also would like to meet China's new musical talents. Perhaps even impart some of the wisdom that comes from composing and performing for more than half a century.

I should also point out other members of the Chinese delegation have also asked for us to perform *Sunset Glow*, but that may have to wait for another trip. It is a good play suitable for young and old, but it requires numerous performances and a large production budget."

Chapter 42.

Celebrating Minorities

庆祝少数民族

Ma's final work, the Opera Rebia (le-be-ya), took ten years to complete.

In winter 1964, a friend mailed me a long poetry book with drawings of an epic nineteenth-century Uyghur love story entitled *Rebia and Saiding.*

A 15-year-old Uyghur peasant girl named Rebia and a 16-year-old Uyghur lad named Saiding fell in love at first sight and eventually planned to marry. But when the time came, the impoverished Saiding could not afford the marriage betrothals. Since the man was the undisputed boss in Uyghur families, Rebia's old-fashioned father convinced a wealthy merchant Ximudei to snatch her away from Saiding's tender heart. Ximudei had Saiding shot and killed by his domestic servant. The unbearable news caused the despairing Rebia to commit suicide by drowning herself in the Qin River.

~

My daughter Celia felt the story and the three drawings—happy Rebia on a balcony above Saiding, pained Rebia in a bridal dress, and distraught Rebia running toward her death in the river—were enchanting and dramatic.

"Father," said Celia one night over dinner, "have you thought about *our* story? I think it would make a beautiful opera."

I smiled at her boldness—she had so much of Muli's fire. "Little one, what do you know about composing an opera?"

"Nothing," she said. "But I can learn; I would have the best teacher in the whole world." Soon after that, the Cultural Revolution happened, and everything changed. The story was sharply at odds with Mao's teachings that peasant minorities such as the Uyghurs were not indigenous Chinese and should therefore be kept in their place, not glorified.

I warned Celia, "My daughter, if we work on this project, it must be for our satisfaction because if such a work were ever made public in China, our family and friends would be in grave jeopardy. Now is not the right time."

~

As you've read, my family and I managed to escape China and begin a busy, fulfilling new life in America. One evening after dinner, Celia reminded me of *Rebia and Saiding.* "My daughter, I'm not convinced I wanted to work on an opera with my talented but undisciplined daughter." Celia would not take no for an answer, so we compromised. I suggested we create a song called *Rebia* with the same feelings as the opera might have. Soon, Celia decided to attend a concert of my music in Taiwan while I toured and performed in the States. Celia spoke to friends in the Twianese musical elite, simplified the lyrics to sound like the vocal cadence in a folk song, and persuaded a talented soprano named Liu Yun to include the music in her performance. *Rebia* received an enthusiastic audience and critical response. I only discovered this when I received a glowing letter from a friend in Taiwan who attended the concert.

~

I could not let Celia's passion and enthusiasm fade. Over the next 12 months, Celia and I composed a major opera based on the ancient story. When the first draft was complete, we entitled it *Love Song Under Ice-Capped Mountain*. During the opera's development, I tried to provide a conceptual direction. My argumentative daughter replied, "That doesn't help; give me examples."

I was blunt. "The male character is more like a tour guide than a lover, the title is wrong, and the script does not command audience involvement from start to finish." Celia decided my comments were too harsh. Muli took Celia's side. I decided to let my creative actions speak for me rather than battle two strong-willed women in the same household. Eventually, Celia recognized her shortcomings and started to research why American musical dramas were so successful. In the process, Celia agreed to rename the work *Rebia*.

~

When we finished the first draft, I knew it still needed work.

But our reconciliation with China had just become official, so I felt it was now safe to travel anywhere without the concern of political retribution or extradition. I suggested to Muli this might be an excellent time to take a break from composing and take a leisurely trip through parts of Europe. Muli's strong reaction surprised me.

"Ma, we have traveled our whole life; now is the time to stay home and enjoy the grandkids. We are not getting any younger."

I decided to do what all mature American husbands do—I implored and begged! Muli finally weakened. "I agree under one condition. No music compositions, no sheet music, and no violin. Just you and me."

We visited Belgium, Austria, Germany, Italy, France, Sweden, Yugoslavia, and England during June and quickly developed a daily routine. We'd get up at 5:00 or 6:00 A.M., have breakfast and write postcards to the children back home, put in a full day exploring new things, and then go to bed pleasantly exhausted by about 10:00 P.M.

When we returned home, the entire family met us at the airport. My son-in-law, Ken, asked, "Father, you look in good spirits despite the long trip. How do you feel?"

I knew he was referring to the shortness of breath episodes I experienced before we left. I again let my actions speak for myself; I leaned over and stretched my arms out so that my granddaughters, Ida and Nina, could run around and give me a big hug. Then I picked up Nina and carried her in my arms to the baggage claim with no difficulty. I smiled at Muli. "Not bad for a 75-year-old man."

~

In early November, without my knowledge or blessing, Celia decided to visit Taiwan, where she was greeted warmly by the Minister of Council for Cultural Affairs, Chen Chi-Li. Celia told him she and I had finished a major new opera called *Rebia,* based on the well-known Uyghur love story, *Rebia, and Saiding.* Celia said the minister hoped to perform the world premiere in Taiwan the following October. Since Taiwan was known as a melting pot of indigenous people living side by side with former Chinese mainlanders, the minister was elated with our interest in premiering the opera in Taiwan and readily agreed to advance 100 percent of the production costs.

When Celia returned home, she told me what she had done. I was unhappy and embarrassed. "Why did you say *Rebia* was finished?"

Celia was upset, "Because that's what you said before you went to Europe!"

"I only said that to make you feel good. *Rebia* is nothing more than a first draft! It's far from done. And I don't know how many times I need to make revisions until I am satisfied. We will not premiere anything in Taiwan that does not meet my standards." Celia walked away in tears; I realized I had treated her too harshly.

Soon, an anxious Minister Chen started asking for the script since he had committed to the October premiere. I knew I could not disappoint my daughter or the minister, so I worked day and night diligently, seven days a week, sometimes skipping doctor appointments, meals, and even sleep. I remember writing in my diary, "At my age, I have two choices: stop working and take life easy, or keep working and risk death. I prefer the latter."

As I continued to work, I began to experience sharp pain in my left leg; sometimes, it was so severe I couldn't sleep. Odd-shaped blisters also started to appear on my skin. Muli insisted we visit the doctor, who quickly diagnosed me with an aggressive virus that invades bodies with weak immune systems. The doctor said it was not fatal, but there was no quick cure. I needed lots of rest and regular vitamin B-12 injections to boost my immune system. I asked if there were any side effects of the injections. He replied, "Just one. If you do nothing, the virus will cause irreparable damage to your heart.

I tried to follow the doctor's orders. By Christmas, *Rebia* was completed, but I was physically and emotionally exhausted. It felt like I had just crossed the finish line of a long marathon race.

Chapter 43.

My Last Days with Family

我最後同家人的日子

(l -r) The Ma family. Ma, Muli, Celia, Ida, Ken and Nina in rear.

Without warning, I suddenly contracted a heavy chest cold and a 103-degree fever. Yet, I was reluctant to see another doctor. I figured I could nurse myself back to health.

Ken disagreed. "Father, people with severe colds should seek medical attention. Particularly at your age."

"I'm not old," I responded indignantly.

"Father, you are almost 75 years. At least talk to the doctor on the telephone."

After hearing my symptoms, my doctor ordered me to the emergency room, quickly diagnosed me with pneumonia and irregular heart rhythm. I was asked to remain in the hospital for observation. During a family visit the following day, I began to experience a burning sensation throughout my body. The intravenously-administered antibiotics had accidentally dripped out of my veins and into my blood vessels. Soon, I needed oxygen to assist my breathing. Ken tried to comfort me, "Papa, you look good; you will recover soon."

I replied, "My son-in-law, thank you for the inspirational diagnosis, but pneumonia is scary; many people die from this."

Ida also tried to cheer me up. "Grandpa, you should be pleased. You were the first one to ride in my car the day after I got my driver's license."

I smiled, "I guess riding with an untested driver is safer than sitting in a hospital with pneumonia."

Muli shook her head. "At least my husband has not lost his sense of humor. He is becoming more American each day."

~

I was released from the hospital three days later, but I knew my health was not getting better. After a short walk to the bathroom, I sat on the edge of the bed to catch my breath. I didn't want anybody to worry, so I tried to make small talk when I went into the living room for dinner. "I've not read a newspaper for days; how is the political situation on the mainland?"

"Good," said Muli. "The Deng government appears open to change."

"Then the day is coming when we will finally be able to go home, " I replied.

"Not so quickly," responded Muli. "After what we have experienced, I remain only cautiously optimistic."

Coincidentally, Muli's younger sister, a nurse, called. Muli described my shortness of breath and noticed the color of my lips changing for the first time. Her sister said, "Get Ma to the hospital right now!"

~

By the time Celia and Ken arrived at the hospital, I had been diagnosed with acute edema and placed in the Intensive Care Unit at the Medical College of Pennsylvania (MCP), where I received several extreme resuscitation measures by the coronary care unit team.

By now, my heart was beating like a drum, and I had to be sedated. The doctors told Muli and me that my best solution for long-term recovery was immediate heart surgery. I explained to Muli, "I know they have best intentions, but, for the first time in a long time, I am pain-free, and my appetite has returned." Muli and I decided I should be discharged so that I could recuperate at home. The doctors disagreed with our immediate decision, but we did agree to schedule further tests to identify the extent of my heart damage.

I knew I had made the right decision as soon as we got home. My little six-year-old granddaughter Nina jumped into my lap, gave me a big hug, and said, "Gung Gung [my nickname], let's play." We had great fun, but I quickly tired. I kissed Nina, then retired to the bedroom to rest and listen to Beethoven's Fifth Symphony with Muli by my side. As she held me in her arms, I cried uncontrollably. Some were tears of happiness for my life's accomplishments, and some were tears of sadness for the pain and suffering my friends and family had experienced because of me.

~

My son-in-law was about to go on a business trip for his new Employer, National Gypsum. We agreed that if the doctor's tests suggested heart surgery was necessary, we would wait till Ken returned.

The day after this latest group of tests, Celia called Muli to find out the results. We were told that my heart condition was *too severe* for surgery. Celia, Muli, and I were confused. Our first instinct was to create our own heart healing medicine by combining western and Chinese herbal medications and counseling.

Ken disagreed. "Philadelphia has some of the best doctors and hospitals in the world. We should take advantage of their knowledge and wisdom." Ken phoned the chief cardiologist, who explained,

" Your father-in-law's two left ventricular valves are not functioning properly—one is leaking, the other is badly calcified."

Ken delivered the bad news in person, "Father, the doctor insists you must have the surgery to replace the two valves. If you do not, you will not live past this year. And if pneumonia returns, your condition will deteriorate even faster, ultimately requiring round-the-clock caregivers."

"I understand," I replied. "Would you please tell Mother?" When Muli received the news, she became frightened that something unforeseen might happen during the surgery.

Ken replied, "The doctor said the success rate is 90-95 percent, which means the surgery is serious but not that dangerous."

Celia said, "I think we would be wise to get a second opinion." Ken did some research. The best hospital for cardiac surgery was the Hospital of the University of Pennsylvania (HUP). I met with the chief cardiologist; his diagnosis was the same as my doctor at Medical College of Pennsylvania.

~

As we drove home, an argument broke out between Muli and Celia. Celia felt heart surgery was not a small matter and should be done at HUP, clearly the best hospital in the area. Ken voiced a similar opinion. Muli glared, "Shouldn't that be your father's decision?"

I became impatient with the bickering, "I have decided to stay the course with my doctor of ten years. I trust him."

There was a moment of silence. Ken looked at Celia, "The choice of a doctor depends on the trust of the patient. If we force our father to go to HUP, and God forbid they fail, how could we ever shoulder that responsibility?"

The recommended pre-surgery regimen at the Medical College of Pennsylvania consisted of rest for three weeks, home checks every few days by a registered nurse, B-12 injections to boost my immune system, and a final pre-op examination. I regained more than ten pounds and much of my positive mental attitude.

As Muli and I sat in the living room, I joked, "After the surgery, I am going to climb the Himalayas."

Muli smiled, "I have some good news for when you come down the mountain. Celia has heard from the Minister of Culture; he loves the final script for *Rebia*. The plan is to stage the production next March in Taipei."

~

The day before surgery, my jaw started to ache. The dentist said I had three inflamed teeth, and they should be removed to avoid unforeseen surprises during heart surgery. My cardiologist agreed, and the surgery was rescheduled for the following week. Although I was disappointed, my doctor's meticulous caring boosted everybody's confidence that I had made the right choice in surgeons.

The dentist very skillfully removed those teeth in the morning, and we all went home for the weekend. Julon bought a beautiful violin; Ken and Celia went to Chinatown to buy some of my favorite Dim Sum varieties. After dinner, I performed Schubert's *Serenade*, filling our apartment with memories of our happy, marvelous days together.

~

On Sunday, Celia returned with Ida and Nina. "Nina does not know when she will see you again, so she brought a painting for you," smiled Celia. Nina jumped into my arms and proudly showed her painting. "For you, Gung Gung." I laughed out loud and kissed her again and again.

~

Monday, I was readmitted to complete the required pre-operation tests. Since I knew there would be waits between results, I asked Muli to bring the *Rebia* script. "Ma, I don't understand. The Minister has approved the script."

I replied, "My work can always be improved. There is time before the premiere."

Muli just shook her head; after all the years together, she knew "good enough" was never actually good enough for me.

~

The scheduled two-hour exam took four hours, which concerned everyone. When the doctor returned with the results, he told my family, "We didn't expect Mu's blood vessels to be so twisted, so they had to take more time to make sure we were properly functioning for the surgery."

Muli asked if I minded that she left early. "Remember, today Ida receives a special award at school. I would like to be there with Celia." I told her, "Family was our most important gift. Go, enjoy."

As the hours passed, I became increasingly anxious about the next day. I called Muli to make small talk. The second call was around midnight. She heard the concern in my voice. "Ma, you are in good hands. Remember, the success rate is 95 percent. Celia wanted me to tell you that when you are fully recovered, we are all going to take a long trip to celebrate."

The following day, I called Muli before I went into surgery to ask a favor. "When I come out of surgery, please squeeze my hand three times to wake me from the sedation."

I could feel her smile on the phone. "Dear husband, I will squeeze your hand as long as it takes to wake you up." Three hours later, the doctor called Muli to tell her the surgery went well, and she, in turn, called Celia with the good news.

Hours went by. There were no further updates on my status. Celia was beside herself; she kept calling the hospital until she reached an evening nurse on the surgery floor. "All I know is your father is still in surgery."

Celia called again, trying to get someone who knew more. The person on the other end of the phone said, "Your father has just left the surgery."

Celia pleaded for more information. "I don't know anything more, but here is a special number to contact the team directly." She called the number. The voice whispered hurriedly, "Your father's condition is unstable, but we are doing everything we can to save him."

Celia was inconsolable as her teenage daughter slept by her side. Celia took two sedatives and then lay in bed, staring at the ceiling. The phone rang; it was Third Aunt. "You must go to the hospital right now. Our good friend Weixiong is on the way to pick you up."

Ida awoke. "Mommy, is everything all right?"

"Ida, Mommy has to see Grandfather at the hospital. I'll call you when the time is right."

~

As Celia and Weixiong drove to the hospital, it started to rain hard. The road became slippery; visibility was about five feet. "Don't worry," said Weixiong, "I will keep you safe in this terrible storm."

They reached the hospital gate about 1:00 A.M., which was locked. Celia, now soaking wet, found a way to enter through an unmarked side door. She found the waiting room and entered. The room was so poorly lit she could barely make out Muli, Third Aunt, and Julon in the corner. Celia sat next to my trembling Muli and held her hand tight.

The air was so heavy the room felt suffocating. Time was frozen. Celia prayed, "God, save him! Save him! Please save him!"

~

As I lay still on the operating room table, I imagined walking toward a bright yellow light. Along the way, I passed through a serene forest, alive with color and the sounds of nature. The leaves were so moist I could see the dewdrops. As I walked further, I came upon a dramatic landscape of granite peaks and mist-shrouded valleys. There, at the base of a thousand-year-old flat-crowned Greeting Pine Tree, sat a violin. I picked it up and began to play *Song of the Mountain Forest*. My heart was 18 years old again. When I finished, I returned the violin to the tree, and the dark silence of night filled the air.

~

The door to the operating room opened several times, with doctors and nurses providing Muli and Celia with brief updates. Finally, the chief cardiologist entered. "We have tried everything, but his blood pressure is too low to do much. I think this might be the time to see him."

Muli sat paralyzed. Julon and Third Aunt entered the intensive care room. There were many tubes with hanging bottles attached to my still body.

An irrational Celia started screaming at the top of her lungs. "They have given up. We should go find another hospital and another doctor before it's too late!" She stared at Weixiong. "Why don't you do something? Call Kai Kai (Ken's nickname); he always knows what to do. And let's find friends; maybe they can come up with new ideas." Celia sat and wept until she was exhausted.

Soon, the nurse came out of my room and said, "He is gone." She asked my family if they would like to see me for the last time. The nurse lifted the white cloth covering me.

"He looks like he is in a deep, peaceful sleep," said a deeply saddened Muli. "He was my whole world." Celia was frozen, speechless. They all huddled together and embraced tightly.

Muli looked at the tubes dangling from my body. She screamed, "Take those tubes out. All of them!" Muli turned and asked, "How could this be? Am I in a terrible dream?" She was unable to accept what had happened.

Third aunt tried to calm Muli. "Take another look. Then I think it's time for us to go home."

Muli gently raised my eyelids to say goodbye, and then she soothed my whole body with her gentle touch. Celia did likewise. "Father's body is still warm!" she shouted.

An angry Muli again cried out. "You didn't try hard enough; he wasn't dead!"

~

The nurse remained calm. She understood grief. She looked at Weixiong. "What would you like us to do with the body?"

"Cremation," Muli said without hesitation. "I want to bring my husband back home with me."

When Celia arrived home, Ida opened the door. Celia said, "Gung Gung died!" Ida didn't believe what she had just heard.

Celia then called Ken. "Papa has died!"

Ken was bitter and angry, "They lied. They said the success rate was 95 percent."

Celia asked, "Can you come back right away? Third Aunt, Mommy, and Julon do not know what to do. We wait for you to arrange things."

Afterword

后记

By Cheng Ken Chi, Ph.D.

Ken (left), daughters Nina and Ida, their children, CeCe, Lana, and Ava, and Nina's husband Erik (rear)

My father-in-law has been gone for more than 33 years, but he still lives vividly in my heart.

His elegance, wealth of knowledge, and uncommon humility impressed me deeply. But his tranquil mind is what I most treasured. Ma was a shy man who didn't seek the spotlight. His goal in life was to create the most beautiful Chinese music in the world. Hundreds of millions of Chinese people, and I believe he achieved that goal.

While Ma never sought fame or fortune, fate and circumstance placed him in the middle of many controversial events—all of which he handled with grace and dignity.

As a composer, Ma was a meticulous perfectionist. Every music syllable was essential to him; a work was never complete until every syllable was in the right place. Of his last two pieces, the dramatic dance *Sunset Glow* took six years and eight scripts to complete, and his opera *Rebia* took ten years and numerous revisions.

As an educator, Ma built Central Conservatory Music from the ground up. It has trained many young Asian musicians who went on to play important roles in the world musical stages. Today, the Conservatory still uses teaching methods Ma established to train young talents.

Ma was also a strong supporter of the common people. He adapted many local folk songs into his music; he called them "his music lifeline." My father-in-law felt Chinese composers were very fortunate to have a 5,000-year history and a vast homeland with many diverse cultures that offered the composer unlimited opportunity for inspiration if they took the time and effort to digest them properly.

Ma was a musical deity—an enormously gifted violinist, composer, and educator in my people's minds. But in our relatives' minds, he was just an unselfish husband, father, and grandfather, filled with abundant love of family. We are so grateful to have had him in our lives.

While many incidents describe Ma, the man, one sticks out above many others. On September 13, 1957, Ma and Muli rushed back from their tour of Shanghai to greet the famous Russian violinist David Oistrakh in Shanghai and, days later, to attend his concert in Peking.

Oistrakh's program contained many classic pieces, including Bach's *Concerto* and Prokofiev's *Romeo and Juliet*. Oistrakh's performance was skillful and flawless, and the audience offered thunderous applause in the hope of an encore. Oistrakh announced he would play Ma's *Pastorale*. Oistrakh stood on stage and pointed to Ma to express his greeting. The audience turned their heads to Ma and applauded. Ma was surprised and embarrassed; he did not know how to express himself. After a long pause, Ma stood up and bowed his head. When Oistrakh finished the piece, he once again pointed to Ma. The audience applauded and stamped their feet. This time, Ma quickly stood up and recognized the audience in his shy, dignified manner. Embarrassed by the attention, he never spoke of the incident with the press or at home with the family.

~

Finally, I hope you enjoyed our book. I would thank my good friend and accomplished author Mathew Crisci, who willingly co-write Ma Sicong's life with me. I am a novice in writing, and Mr. Crisci patiently guided me through the process. Without his skill and assistance, presenting this book to readers would not have been possible. My indebtedness to him is unmeasurable.

Ma's Photo Album

马的相簿

The following pages allow you to walk through some of the
highlights of Ma's bittersweet life in photographs
not included in the body of this work.

1923: Ma, 13, and two older brothers,
Siqui and Siwu study in France.

1930: At the age of 18, Ma is declared a musical prodigy,
and composes and performs in Europe.

1931-32: The handsome young Ma becomes
a classical music rock star to the heavily female audiences.

1932: Yat-sen Memorial Hall Guangzhou.
Ma's mother hears him perform in public for the first time.

1933: Ma meets Muli, and they fall in love, against the advice of Ma's mother.

1935: Ma and Muli perform together for the first time at the home of friends in Shanghai.

1936: Ma and musician friends sympathetic to Chiang Kai-shek.

1938: Ma performs *Nostalgia*
in the uniform of Chinese man-fashion of the day.

1940: Ma performs for the soldiers during the Sino-Japanese war.

1941: Ma performs for the soldiers during the Sino-Japanese war.

1945: Meets with his friend, the celebrated poet, Bin Jai.

1951. Ma composing music in his Beijing study.

1954: Ma and Muli visit Mother Huang
at the family home in Haifeng.

1955: Ma meets with Zhou Enlai.

1956: Ma performs publicly for the first time with son, Julon.

1958: Ma performs at the Yat-sen Memorial Hall.

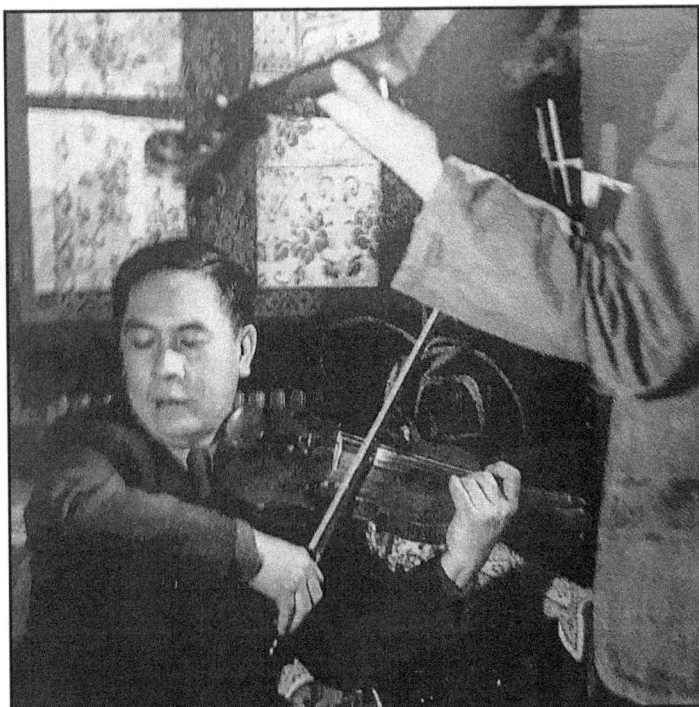

1962: Ma teaches one of his students
in a casual Beijing tea room.

1967: Ma's friends are publicly humiliated
by the cultural revolution for being too Western.

1967: Intellectual humiliations led by the Red Guard.

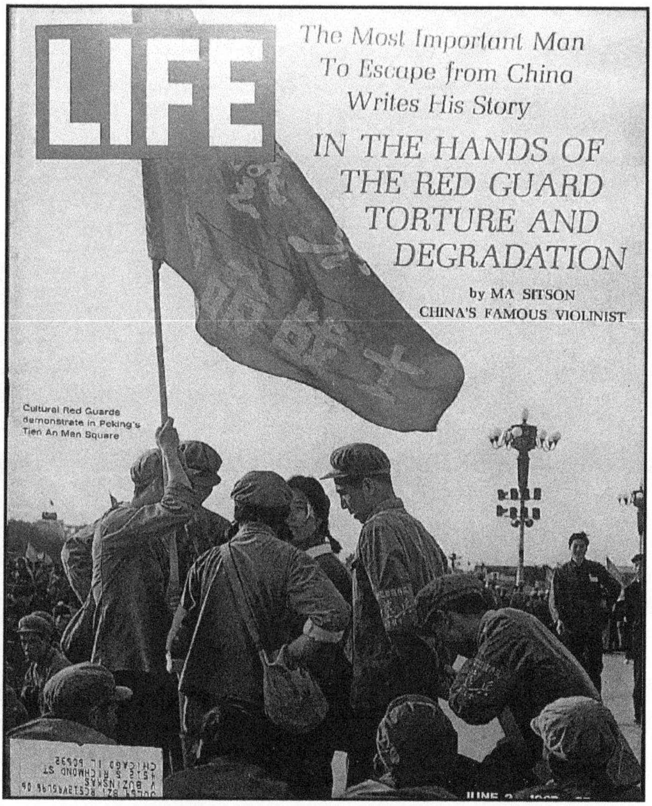

The Most Important Man
To Escape from China
Writes His Story

**IN THE HANDS OF
THE RED GUARD
TORTURE AND
DEGRADATION**

by MA SITSON
CHINA'S FAMOUS VIOLINIST

Cultural Red Guards
demonstrate in Peking's
Tien An Man Square

1967: Ma escapes to the United States,
and lives to write about it for *Life Magazine*.

1972: America assigns CIA operative, Bill Clothier (left), to watch over Ma and his family.

1972: Ma performs at Lincoln Center in New York for the first time.

1973: Ma is awarded a key to the city of Los Angeles.

1974: Muli and Ma don the robes of
Taiwanese aboriginals, the A-Mei.

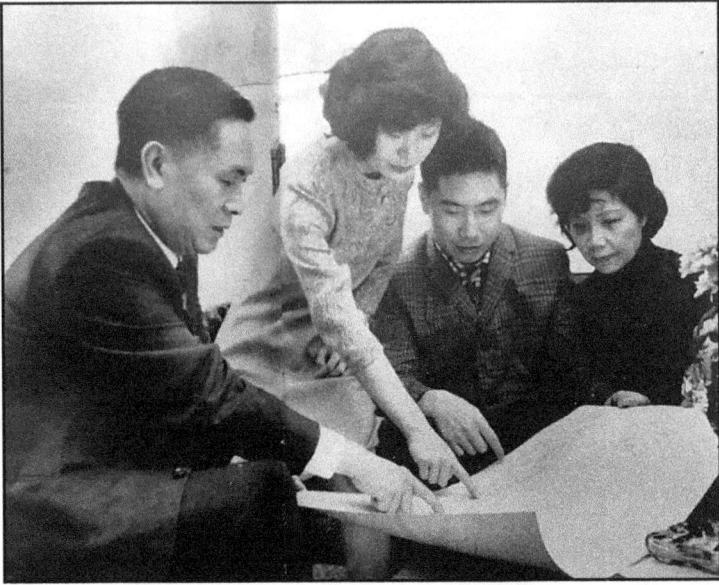

1975: Ma and his family share escape with the American press.

1978: Daughter Celia playing piano at Ma and Muli's home in Philadelphia. Brother Julon watches.

1978: Ma is greeted by Taipei by President Chiang Ching-Kuo, son of deceased Chiang Kai-shek.

1981: Ma in Taipei with lead performers after world premiere of Sunset Glow (*A Romance in Drogan Place*).

1982: Ma and Muli with grandchildren, Ida and baby Nina, in their favorite Philadelphia restaurant.

1987: Private funeral service at Washington Memorial Park Hall joined friends and relatives (right-brother Si-Hon).

1987: One week after the private funeral,
a public memorial service in Manhattan, attended by thousands.

1988: Younger brother, Ma Si-Hon, performs
Violin Concerto in F Major at Ma's memorial concert, Beijing.

1990: Performance of *Rebia* at Sun Yat-sen Memorial Hall, Taiwan with Ma's daughter Celia.

1990. Sold-out memorial concert at Avery Fisher Hall, Lincoln Center, New York.

1990: Ma's dramatic dance, *Sunset Glow,* is staged six times at Tianqiao Theatre, Beijing, as a posthumous tribute.

1997: Celia and granddaughters, Nina and Ida, at Ma's Tenth Anniversary Concert at Rockefeller Center in New York.

2002: Ma Sicong Memorial Hall opens at the world-famous Guangzhou Museum of Art.

2002: Ma's bust and piano are given a place of honor at Ma Sicong Memorial Hall.

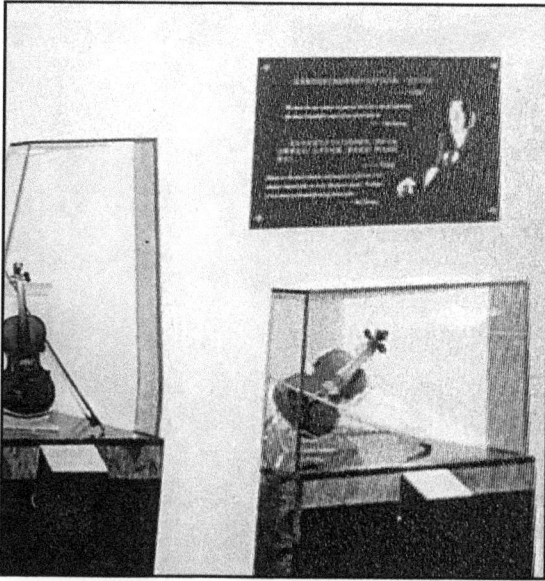

2002. Ma's violin is featured in the museum catalog and an accompanying exhibition.

2007. Ceremony at Washington Memorial Park for sending Ma and Muli's ashes back to Guangzhou.

2007: Ma and Muli's ashes are brought back to Guangzhou by granddaughters Ida, Nina, and son Julon.

2010: Ken and Nina at Ma's wall erected in his home town of Haifeng.

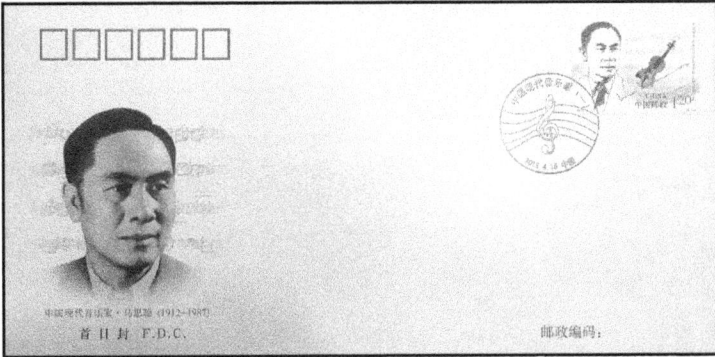

2012: Ma becomes the face of a commemorative stamp and envelope
throughout the Peoples Republic of China.

2012: Ida and Nina visit grandfather's museum exhibit.

2017: The construction of a bronze memorial and tranquility garden is proposed by Museum officials.

References

BOOKS

Chi, Ken. *Ma Sciong Personal Diaries, 1930 – 1986*. Chi Family archives, 2019

Barmouin Barbara and Changgen, Yu. *Zhou Enlai: A Political Life*. Chinese University of Hong King Press, 2006.

Lee, Chae-jin. *Zhou Enlai: The Early Years*. Stanford University Press, 1994.

Reynolds, Stuart. *Mao's Road to Power*. M.E. Sharpe, 1992. Print.

Zedong, Mao. *On New Democracy*. Red Guard Press, 1967.

Dabringhaus, Sabine. **The Monarch and Inner/Outer Court Dualism in Late Imperial China**. Brill Publishing, 2011.

Duindam, Jeroen, editor. *Royal Courts in Dynastic States and Empires. A Global Perspective*. Brill Publishing, 2011.

Rudd, Kevin. *Not for the Faint-Hearted. Zhou Enlai*. Macmillan Publishers, 2017.

Gao, Wenqian. *Zhou Enlai: The Last Perfect Revolutionary*. Perescus Books Group, 2007.

Sheila Melvin and Cai, Jingdong. *Rapsody in Red: How Western Classical Music Became Chinese*. Algora Publishing, 2004.

Suleski, Ronald. *Daily Life for the Common People of China 1850-1950*. Brill Publishing, 2018.

Jie, Jin. *Chinese Music*. Cambridge University Press, 2011.

Zedong, Mao. *Quotations from Chairman Mao Zedong. (The Little Red Book)*. University of Michigan Press, 1966.

Leese, Daniel. *Revolution: Conceptualizing Political and Social Change in the Late Qing Dynasty.* Oriens Extremus, vol. 51..

Explorations in Economic History, vol. 63.
Tsang, Steve. *A Modern History of Hong Kong.* I.B. Tauris & Co. Ltd., 2004

Gray, Jack. *Rebellions and Revolutions: China from the 1800s to 2000.* Oxford University Press, 2002.

Xiaobo Lü, Xiaobo. *Cadres and Corruption: The Organizational Involution of the Chinese Communist Party.* Stanford University Press, 2000.

Rice, Edward. *Mao's Way.* University of California Press. 1974.
Liu, Jingzhi. *A Critical History of New Music in China.* Commercial Press, 1987.

SDhung, Shun yi Taiwan yuan zhu min bo wu guan. *Studies in the History and Culture of the Taiwan Indigenous People.* The Museum of Formosan Aborigines, 2001.

Yonglie, Ye. *A Patriotic Traitor.* Wen Hui Publishing, 2014.

Van de Ven., Hans. *War and Nationalism in China: 1925-1945.* Curzon, London, 2003.

Taylor, Jay. *The Generalmissimo: Chaing Kai-shek and the Struggle for Modern China.* Harvard University Press, 2010. Print.

Meisner, Maurice. *Mao Zedong: A Political and Intellectual Portrait.* Wiley Publishing, 2006.

Sainsbury, Keith. *The Turning Point: Roosevelt, Stalin, Churchill and Chiang Kai-shek, 1943.* Oxford University Press, 1985.

Voegel, Ezra. *Deng Xiaoping and the Transformation of China.* Belnap, Harvard University Press, 2011.

Deng, Xiaoping. *Selected Works of Deng Xiaoping, Part Two: 1982-1992.* Bureau of Translation of the Chinese Communist Party Central Committee. 1997.

Evans, Richard. Deng Xiaoping and the Making of Modern China. Viking Books, 1993.

Run, Mao Yu. *Music Under Mao, Its Background and Aftermath.* University of Texas Press, 1991.

Thien, Madeleine *After the Cultural Revolution: What Western Classical Music Means in China.* The Guardian Press, 2016.

Westad, Odd Arne. *Decisive Encounters: The Chinese Civil War, 1946-1950.* Stanford University Press, 2003.

Hsiu7ng, James. *China's Bitter Victory: The War with Japan, 1937-1945.* M.E. Sharp Publishing, 1992.

Chang, H.H. *Chiang Kai-shek-Asia's Man of Destiny.* Doubleday, 2007.

Cheek, Timothy. *Mao Zedong and China's Revolutions.* Bedford Press Series in History, 2002.

Schram, Stuart. *The Political Thought of Mao Zedong.* Praeger Publishers, 1971.

Stein, R.A. *Tibetan Civilization.* Faber & Faber, London, 1972.

Hsu, Amis et al. *Taiwanese Aboriginal History.* Taipei Press, 2001.

Winckler, Edwin. *Cultural Change in Post War Taiwan.* Westview Press, Boulder, CO., 1994.

Yu, Kang. *Ma Sicong's Cello Concerto in A minor: Analytical Study of This Concerto.* The University of Indiana Doctoral Papers, 2015.

Sicong, Ma. *The Complete Works of Ma Sicong.* Central Conservatory of Music Press, Beijing, 2007. ISBN 9787810962391.

ARTICLES

"In the Hands of the Red Guard Torture and Degradation," Ma Sicong, Life Magazine, 1967.

"China and the West: Imperialism, Opium, and Self-Strengthening," Asia for Educators.

"Ma Sicong Sentenced to Exile." Music Tales, 2019.
https://musictales.club/article/ma-sicong-sentenced-exile-after-seeking-chinese-harmony-his-violin

"Ma Sciong. The Communist Party Version." https://www.wikipedia.org/

http://afe.easia.columbia.edu/main_pop/kpct/kp_imperialism.htm

"The 1911 Revolution and the Frontier Game,."
https://apjjf.org/2014/12/5/FenJianyong/4071/article.html

"Chinese Footbinding," Tiffany Marie Smith.
https://www.britannica.com/science/footbinding

"Foreign Imperialism in China," Jennifer Llewellyn and Glen Kucha.
https://alphahistory.com/chineserevolution/foreign-imperialism-in-china/

"The Butterfly Lovers: A Classic Chinese Love Story."
https://www.medievalists.net/2018/02/butterfly-lovers-classic-chinese-love-story/

"Warlords and Military Cliques in the Warlord Period," https://www.wikipedia.org/

"The Warlords."
https://en.wikipedia.org/wiki/List_of_warlords_and_militarycliques_in_the_Warlord_Era

"The Communist Party of China and the Party-State," Ming XIA. 2008.

"Chaing Kai-shek is dead in Taipei at 87."
https://www.nytimes.com/1975/04/06/archives/chiang-kaishek-is-dead-in-taipei-at-87-last-of-allied-big-four-of.html

"The Culture of Taiwan."
https://en.wikipedia.org/wiki/Culture_of_Taiwan

" Amis People."
https://en.wikipedia.org/wiki/Amis_people

"Taiwanese Indigenous Peoples." Wikipedia.org
https://en.wikipedia.org/wiki/Amis_people

"Chiang Kai-shek," Wikipediia.org
https://en.wikipedia.org/wiki/Chiang_Kai-shek

"What Western Classical Music Means in China."
https://www.theguardian.com/music/2016/jul/08/after-the-cultural-revolution-what-western-classical-music-means-in-china

"Chairman Mao's Talk to Music Workers, 1956.
https://www.marxists.org/reference/archive/mao/selected-works/volume-7/mswv7_469.htm

"Long Live Mao Zedong Thought,"
https://www.marxists.org/subject/china/peking-review/1966/PR1966-27a.htm

"Chronology of Mass Killings during the Chinese Cultural Revolution."
 https://www.marxists.org/subject/china/peking-review/1966/PR1966-27a.htm

"W. Clothier 2nd, Sportsman, Spy."
https://www.beautyman.com/USIC/news/clothier.htm

"Chinese Civil War."
https://en.wikipedia.org/wiki/Chinese_Civil_War#References

"Rapprochement with China, 1972."
https://history.state.gov/milestones/1969-1976/rapprochement-china

"Henry Kissinger's Secret Trip to China.".
https://nsarchive2.gwu.edu/NSAEBB/NSAEBB66/

"Word for Word—Kissinger in China."
https://www.nytimes.com/2002/03/03/weekinreview/word-for-word-kissinger-in-china-beijing-1971-oh-to-be-a-fly-on-the-great-wall.html

"Zhou Enlai."
https://en.wikipedia.org/wiki/Zhou_Enlai

"Mao Zedong's New Democracy,"
https://www.indianfolk.com/mao-zedongs-new-democracy-edited/

"Celebrating the 100th Anniversary of Ma Sicong,"
http://www.bravuraphil.org/2011-12-season/2012-family-concert

"Ma Sicong's Violin Concerto in F Major: Western Tradition and Chinese Elements."
https://scholarworks.iu.edu/dspace/bitstream/handle/2022/20327/Wang%2C%20Yuan%20Yuan%20%28DM%20Violin%29.pdf?sequence

"Ma Sicong Memorial Hall, Guangzhou Museum of Art."
https://www.gzam.com.cn/mrgjs/info_143.aspx?itemid=14650

"Unknown Master Cello Concerto by Ma Sitson"
=0221589939142870 HYPERLINK "https://fsu.catalog.fcla.edu/fs.jsp?
ADV=S&t1=kwang+Yu&k1=au&op1=a&t2=&k2=kw&op2=a&t3=&k3=kw&avli=&fa=&fa=&pf=&pt=&V=D&S=0221589939142870&I=0"

INTERVIEWS

Chin Ken Chi, Ph.D., Laguna Woods, CA

Nina Sabens Chi, Ph.D., Philadelphia, PA

Ida Chi, Ph.D., San Diego, CA

THE WORLD OF
M.G. Crisci
Stories that entertain. People you'll remember. Literature that matters.
mgcrisci.com

Dear Reader,

I wanted to thank you for taking the time to read this book, and I hope you enjoyed the experience. I know life is hectic, and you have many choices.

I was wondering if you might be kind enough to do me one more favor? Post a short review on Amazon.com and goodreads.com.

As you know, reader reviews are more important than ever before. They are how many readers discover and decide to read new books.

My library now includes 16 or so titles, and I've learned many readers make selections after going to those two sites or my website.

Again, thanks for any help you might be willing to provide.

Cordially,

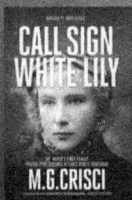

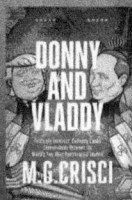

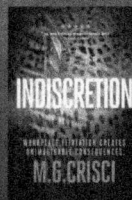

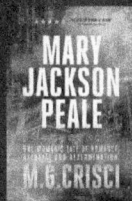

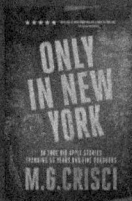

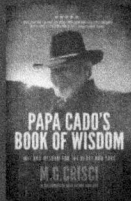

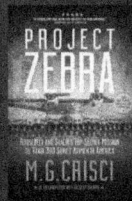

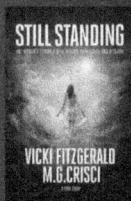

www.ingramcontent.com/pod-product-compliance
Lightning Source LLC
Chambersburg PA
CBHW030409100426
42812CB00028B/2893/J